SHP
HISTORY
YEAR 8

Teacher's
Resource Book

including PDFs on CD-ROM

SHP HISTORY YEAR 8

Teacher's Resource Book
including PDFs on CD-ROM

MAGGIE WILSON
CHRIS CULPIN

HODDER
EDUCATION
AN HACHETTE UK COMPANY

Hachette UK's policy is to use papers that are natural, renewable and recyclable products and made from wood grown in sustainable forests. The logging and manufacturing processes are expected to conform to the environmental regulations of the country of origin.

Orders: please contact Bookpoint Ltd, 130 Milton Park, Abingdon, Oxon OX14 4SB. Telephone: +44 (0)1235 827720. Fax: +44 (0)1235 400454. Lines are open 9.00a.m.–5.00p.m., Monday to Saturday, with a 24-hour message answering service. Visit our website at www.hoddereducation.co.uk

© Maggie Wilson and Chris Culpin 2009
First published in 2009
by Hodder Education, an Hachette UK company
338 Euston Road
London NW1 3BH

Impression number 5 4 3 2 1
Year 2013 2012 2011 2010 2009

Typeset in 11.5/13pt New Baskerville by Phoenix Photosetting, Chatham, Kent
Artwork by Art Construction and Tony Randell
Printed in Great Britain by Hobbs the Printers, Totton, Hants

A catalogue record for this title is available from the British Library

ISBN 978 0340 90737 5

Contents

Introduction

Overview of this course   3

Ten reasons to use this course   4

Key features of the revised National Curriculum   5

How *SHP History* covers the revised National Curriculum   8

Using this material in the classroom – lesson planning issues   15

Assessment   24

LESSON SEQUENCE PLANS

Introduction Overview   27

          1 The book with no name (Pupil's Book pages 2–13)   28

Section 1 Overview   30

          2 Ordinary lives 1500–1750 (Pupil's Book pages 14–23)   31

          3 What did the Industrial Revolution do for us? 1750–1850 (Pupil's Book pages 24–31)   33

          4 A better time for all? Ordinary life 1850–1900 (Pupil's Book pages 32–49)   35

Section 2 Overview   37

          5 The Spanish Empire (Pupil's Book pages 50–65)   38

          6 The British Empire and the slave trade (Pupil's Book pages 66–89) 42

          7 The British Empire (Pupil's Book pages 90–97)   48

Section 3 Overview   51

          8 Movement and settlement into the unknown: were all emigrants brave and adventurous? (Pupil's Book pages 98–111)   52

Section 4 Overview   55

          9 Invasion attempts (Pupil's Book pages 112–129)   56

          10 Which wars? A quick history of war and peace (Pupil's Book pages 130–139)   61

Section 5   Overview   65

    11 Would you have signed Charles I's death warrant?
(Pupil's Book pages 140–149)   66

    12 The Royal Rollercoaster (Pupil's Book pages 150–171)   70

    13 Hero or villain? Why do reputations change over time?
(Pupil's Book pages 172–177)   73

Section 6   Overview   75

    14 How can you change things for the better?
(Pupil's Book pages 178–193)   76

    15 Winning the vote in nineteenth-century Britain
(Pupil's Book pages 194–203)   82

    16 How did the Chartists try to win the vote?
(Pupil's Book pages 204–215)   87

Conclusion   Overview   91

    17 What have you learned this year? (Pupil's Book pages 216–228)   92

Progression in key concepts from Year 7 to Year 8   95

ACTIVITY SHEETS

Introduction: Activity sheets 1–2   96

Section 1: Activity sheets 3–15   98

Section 2: Activity sheets 16–29   113

Section 3: Activity sheets 30–32   129

Section 4: Activity sheets 33–37   134

Section 5: Activity sheets 38–40   140

Section 6: Activity sheets 41–47   150

Conclusion: Activity sheets 48–50   158

Introduction

◆〉 Overview of this course

  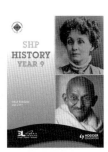

SHP History provides a complete course for KS3 History. It covers the KS3 National Curriculum Programme of Study offering all you would expect from SHP:
- intriguing content
- source-based investigation
- varied learning styles

but combining that with significant new features that reflect the new possibilities and requirements of the revised National Curriculum, in particular focusing on
- big thematic stories across time
- carefully planned progression in historical skills and concepts.

For each year of KS3 the course offers three closely related components:

Pupil's Book

- full colour textbook
- with spacious layout
- containing stunning visuals
- packed full of interesting and worthwhile activities
- offering plenty of flexibility and choice of different pathways for different schools with different approaches to course planning.

Dynamic Learning CD-ROM

- all elements of the Pupil's Book to open, save and manipulate how you wish
- interactive versions of key activities from the Pupil's Book
- additional activities that are suited to ICT applications, e.g. decision-making exercises or PowerPoint-based voting activities
- audio files, recorded by professional actors, for long or important written sources from the Pupil's Book
- a vast resource bank of images for use however you wish
- links to web-based resources
- a Lesson Builder tool that allows you to mix these materials with others of your own to create your own lessons and design your own course.

Teacher's Resource Book

- authoritative advice on the implications of the new curriculum for course planning
- 'lesson sequence' plans outlining starter, development and plenary activities
- photocopiable resource sheets for all major activities
- activity sheets and lesson plans are also included on the CD provided with the Teacher's Resource Book
- links to Thinking History website which provides further support for active learning.

➔ Ten reasons to use this course

Together the books and CD will ensure you can fully meet the statutory requirements of the revised National Curriculum History Programme of Study. You can be confident it covers all the required concepts and processes, and range and content. However, this series is about much more than jumping through a set of statutory hoops. It aims to provide a coherent and pupil-friendly course based on current best practice in History teaching while offering real, practical solutions to the problems that many History teachers face. So here are ten reasons to use this course.

1. **It is based on thorough understanding of the aims of the revised curriculum:** This series has been several years in the making, having been conceived well before the 2008 National Curriculum History Programme of Study was devised. Many aspects of the new Programme of Study are based on ideas developed by SHP over a number of years and trialled with teachers through Inset sessions and in other publications. This series is not a 'quick fix' reaction to the revised Programme of Study but a carefully planned attempt to build around its core ideas and principles.

2. **It provides cross-key-stage coherence:** All sections have been planned to link backwards and forwards across time. All three books/CDs (for Year 7, Year 8 and Year 9) have been planned together to ensure that pupils can see the thematic stories unfold across time and develop their skills progressively across the key stage. Year 8 and Year 9 resources make regular references back to topics covered earlier. The Learning Logs encourage pupils to record what they have learned, in their own way, for future reference across KS3.

3. **It builds the big thematic stories across time:** One of the most important new features in helping to create coherence is the Big Story. Each section focuses on one of the main themes featured in the National Curriculum (movement and settlement, empire, political power, conflict, ordinary life). The Big Story pages build up these stories, year by year, contextualising the enquiry and connecting it to work in later or earlier years. Pupils

summarise developments in their own way to re-use that learning later in KS3. They can also create their own Big Story films using Movie Maker.

4. **It progressively builds pupils' historical skills across the key stage:** The Doing History pages help pupils understand how History is studied. Each concept and process emerges naturally from an enquiry (e.g. 'using evidence' develops from pupils' work on finding out about the Industrial Revolution). They cover the full range of concepts and processes required by the National Curriculum – and which form the basis for assessment. Pupils gradually build up a more complex understanding of these concepts and processes across the series. New challenges appear each year – and by the end of KS3, pupils will have used a full range of processes and concepts which will be a springboard for GCSE success.

5. **It offers pupils a real sense of achievement:** Each of the previous points – the careful planning, the Big Stories and the Doing History features – are all part of a bigger aim: to foster a real sense of achievement. All along we've planned backwards, focusing on what pupils will 'take away' from their KS3 History course. Using this course we hope that pupils will emerge from KS3 with a real sense of achievement: understanding how History is studied and why it is useful, and also able to relate the present to the past. They will be able to tell the Big Stories of ordinary life, empires, etc. at a level appropriate to their abilities. And instead of ending their compulsory History armed with a range of interesting but often isolated details and stories, pupils will have built their own more coherent sense of the past.

6. **It promotes active learning:** Active learning is an essential part of History lessons for a wide range of reasons. It meets the needs of those who learn best through physical activity while providing variety for everyone. It encourages the ability to ask questions and to focus talk, which in turn leads to better thinking and written work. It is a proven way of creating memorable overviews. In addition, a point often missed about active learning is that it enables pupils to handle a greater depth of knowledge and to reach more sophisticated understandings, thus providing more challenge and greater

achievement. Active learning sessions are also often the most memorable and motivating for pupils, a critical element in enabling you to re-use learning later in KS3 by asking, 'Do you remember when ...?' Without that memorability the coherence of courses is much more likely to break down.

7. **It integrates book-based and computer-based learning:** We have planned the Pupil's Book, the Dynamic Learning CD-ROM and the Teacher's Resource Book together, aiming to use each medium for the tasks it does best. For example, you will find decision-making activities on the CD but not in the textbook where they don't work nearly as well. The CD is also the place for voting activities, prediction exercises to identify pupils' ideas and knowledge before they begin a unit of work (formative assessment which helps you guide their learning) and resources to help them record and keep the key points they have covered in each year. At other times the book and CD work in harmony. For example, you can use the long written sources in the Pupil's Book as text or you can support poorer readers with the audio versions from the CD. The CD contains dozens of so-called 'mini-activities' – one-off demonstrations or white board interactive on-screen activities to slot into a lesson to underline a key point. It also offers a range of more ambitious 'maxi-activities' – entire lesson sequences delivered through generic software such as Word, PowerPoint, Excel and Movie Maker, so if you have a computer suite available you can run a much more ICT-driven course.

8. **It offers choices for teachers and personalisation for pupils:** Each school is different, so teachers need choice of method of teaching and choice of pathway through the material. Pupils want choices too. So there is more material in the books and on the CDs than most teachers will use – and that's deliberate. We want to provide you with choices of topic, choice of approach, choice of level of difficulty, choice of learning style. There are also choices to be made by pupils so they can personalise their learning. For example, which aspect of the Spanish Conquest (Section 2, pages 54–59) will each group choose to work on? And there's a choice of learning styles with

opportunities to vary between reading text, listening to audio, taking part in kinaesthetic activities, creating mind maps and many more. The Dynamic Learning CD helps here too. Using the Lesson Builder you can mix together material from different years to construct your scheme of work – for example, you can take the material on empires from each year and create an integrated set of lessons to teach the theme of empires in a single term or across a single year.

9. **It helps you fit the curriculum to the time you have available:** Perhaps the biggest problem some teachers face is time – how do you fit it all in? Schools have vastly differing amounts of teaching time at their disposal but nobody ever feels they have enough. We have tackled the time problem in two ways. Firstly, by providing a variety of outline and depth activities, enabling you to cover outlines quickly and providing frameworks within your depth studies nest. Secondly, we have created activities that can be tackled by groups working on different aspects of a topic, pooling their results to create a bigger answer. This saves time while making sure all pupils maintain their understanding of the big thematic stories.

10. **It offers enjoyment!** Nobody learns if they don't enjoy what they are doing. All the activities, whether in the book or on the CD, have been created to maximise involvement and enjoyment and to help pupils care about the questions they are investigating. And hopefully you will enjoy the material too!

Key features of the revised National Curriculum

The Programme of Study offers the chance to keep what's good (developing pupils' understanding of concepts and processes, creating challenging enquiry questions for in-depth investigations, designing activities that use a variety of learning styles) but highlights the need to do some things better – notably to link the different stages of the course together more coherently and yet at the same time to tailor your course more to your own pupils' interests and needs.

The following are general comments on the key components of the Programme of Study.

Curriculum aims and the importance of History

> History fires pupils' curiosity and imagination, moving and inspiring them with the dilemmas, choices and beliefs of people in the past. It helps pupils develop their own identities through an understanding of history at personal, local, national and international levels. It helps them to ask and answer questions of the present by engaging with the past.
>
> Pupils find out about the history of their community, Britain, Europe and the world. They develop a chronological overview that enables them to make connections within and across different periods and societies. They investigate Britain's relationships with the wider world, and relate past events to the present day.
>
> As they develop their understanding of the nature of historical study, pupils ask and answer important questions, evaluate evidence, identify and analyse different interpretations of the past, and learn to substantiate any arguments and judgements they make. They appreciate why they are learning what they are learning and can debate its significance.
>
> History prepares pupils for the future, equipping them with knowledge and skills that are prized in adult life, enhancing employability and developing an ability to take part in a democratic society. It encourages mutual understanding of the historic origins of our ethnic and cultural diversity, and helps pupils become confident and questioning individuals.
>
> *National Curriculum Statement on curriculum aims and the importance of History*

The introductory statement is easily skipped over but it's of major importance in defining what we're trying to do in History and in putting the pupils' needs at the forefront of the Programme of Study. It is wonderful to see phrases referring to children's enjoyment of History, to their curiosity and imagination being fired, to their being able to ask and answer questions of the present by engagement with the past.

Concepts and processes

- Chronological understanding
- Cultural, ethnic and religious diversity
- Change and continuity
- Cause and consequence
- Significance
- Interpretation
- Historical enquiry
- Using evidence
- Communicating about the past

The list of concepts and processes is broadly familiar with the exception of 'Cultural, ethnic and religious diversity', which doesn't immediately look like one of the second-order concepts we are used to. It is easy to argue that pupils need to appreciate how, for example, religious, cultural and ethnic diversities have developed and how this diversity impacts on the world – but this is to treat it more as a content criterion than a second-order concept offering useful routes of progression. The Historical Association has developed guidance material on defining and implementing ideas about diversity which can be found on their website at **www.history.org.uk/Secondary_Key_Stage_3.asp**. If diversity is to be a valid second-order concept we will need to define progression precisely. We think that diversity (as a concept) is fundamentally about helping children to use and to challenge generalisations in History, to appreciate that experiences in time and place have been very different and to be able to represent these differences in their written and oral descriptions of the past. In this sense diversity is closely linked to the concept of interpretations as historical interpretations often differ because their creators have focused on diverse people, experiences or sources. Other concepts have been given greater prominence, notably interpretations and significance. Although much of these concepts and processes are familiar in terms of language there is still a great deal to be done to discover how to develop understandings most effectively.

Range and content

- the development of **political power** from the Middle Ages to the twentieth century
- the different histories and changing relationships through time of the peoples of **England, Ireland, Scotland and Wales**
- the impact through time of the **movement and settlement** of diverse peoples to, from and within the British Isles
- the way in which **the lives**, beliefs, ideas and attitudes **of people in Britain** have changed over time and the factors – such as technology, economic development, war, religion and culture – that have driven these changes
- the development of **trade, colonisation, industrialisation and technology**, the **British Empire** and its impact on different people in Britain and overseas, pre-colonial civilisations, the nature and effects of **the slave trade**, and resistance and decolonisation
- the impact of significant political, social, cultural, religious, technological and/or economic developments and events on past European and world societies
- the changing nature of **conflict and co-operation** between countries and peoples and its lasting impact on national, ethnic, racial, cultural or religious issues, including the nature and impact of the two world wars and the Holocaust, and the role of European and international institutions in resolving conflicts

The most obvious difference in the Programme of Study is the way that content is defined by these 'thematic stories' rather than by chronological period. This is where much of the potential of the Programme of Study lies for creating a more coherent course, although it doesn't mean instant revolution in what you cover or how you structure your courses. You will probably need to continue to teach the staples – 1066, Magna Carta, Black Death, Civil War, etc. – since they are critical elements of the various thematic stories, but the key requirement is that you use those staples to help you build pupils' understanding of a bigger story.

It is worth saying that while the Programme of Study chose (at a rather late stage and for political reasons not educational ones) to divide the themes under two headings – 'British' and 'European and World' – this can be ignored. It will not make for good history and it is much more relevant to focus on the phrase which precedes the themes about making 'appropriate links' between the aspects. It would be quite illogical, for example, to treat empire as a solely British theme or war as solely a European and World one. History across national boundaries produces more interesting, and, we believe, better history for British pupils. This definition of content by thematic story may well prove to be a major advance in helping children develop their historical knowledge and understandings and their sense of chronology.

Curriculum opportunities

- explore the ways in which **the past has helped shape** identities, shared cultures, values and attitudes **today**
- investigate aspects of **personal, family or local history** and how they relate to a broader historical context
- appreciate and evaluate, through visits where possible, the role of **museums**, galleries, archives and **historic sites** in preserving, presenting and influencing people's attitudes towards the past
- **use ICT** to research information about the past, process historical data, and select, categorise, organise and present their findings
- make links between History and **other subjects** and areas of the curriculum, including citizenship

Each of the five elements has a particular role to play and all are welcome. SHP has a particular commitment to local history and to the use of local sites. We comment later in these notes (see page 20) on the strengths and weaknesses of cross-curricular work. Probably the most significant area for development at the moment, however, is in the use of ICT as a means of research, as a mode of teaching and an increasingly sophisticated medium for pupils to record and present their work. Effective use of ICT has been one of the driving forces of this new course. In a quickly changing environment we have not tried to follow the latest techno-gimmick but to identify how ICT can really enhance and benefit historical learning.

All change?

You are not expected to have provided a new, fully-fledged scheme of work by September 2008. The idea is that you build towards that over three years – and even by then you won't have made all the changes you want to make or that are possible to make, especially as there are new GCSE and A level specifications to be introduced. The ideal is to have mapped out a broad plan for your new KS3 scheme of work, to have worked in detail on Year 7 for September 2008 and then to revise the broad plan in the light of how it's going. How fast you go depends on many factors – those new specifications, how much support (or the reverse) you get from your management team, what kind of colleagues you have and how well you work together – not to mention all those domestic issues that take priority over working life. Keep doing what you are already doing well but begin to adapt activities to fit into the new Programme of Study – it could be really exciting!

◆▶ How *SHP History* covers the revised National Curriculum

Overview

The most common way of structuring the KS3 course is to move steadily through time across KS3. We have retained that broadly chronological structure for this new course:
- Year 7 – up to *c.*1500
- Year 8 – *c.*1500–*c.*1900
- Year 9 – mid nineteenth century through to the present.

Within this structure we revisit the main thematic stories in each year.

However, all three books have enquiries that step outside these chronological boundaries and take a longer overview to help pupils consolidate their overall sense of chronology. In particular, the Big Story element spreads well beyond the chronological confines of the period to help contextualise each enquiry and to help link past and present.

Table 1 shows the broad structure of each book, identifying the themes (Big Stories), major enquiry questions and the conceptual focus of each enquiry. The italic shows enquiries that include rapid overviews. There are more detailed overviews of the Big Stories and conceptual focus in Tables 2 and 3.

Table 1: Overview of the series

Big Stories across time	Major enquiries in Y7	Conceptual focus	Major enquiries in Y8	Conceptual focus	Major enquiries in Y9	Conceptual focus
	• The mystery of the skeletons	What is History Evidence Enquiry				
Movement and settlement	• *Quick history: Romans to Normans – who made the biggest difference?*	Chronology	• Were all emigrants brave and adventurous?	Diversity and generalisation	• How should the story of immigration be told?	Diversity
Empires	• Did people love or hate living in the Roman Empire?	Diversity Interpretations	• Why were Europeans mad about empires?	Interpretations	• Why is the British Empire so controversial?	Interpretations
Conflict … and co-operation	• Who told the truth about 1066? • What should everyone know about the Crusades?	Evidence	• Which wars should we know about?	Significance Causes	• How did people respond to wars in 1914 and 1939? • Why did attempts to stop the Second World War fail? • Why is it so hard to achieve peace in the Middle East?	Causes and Consequences
Ordinary life – what was it like?	• Was it all muck and misery in the Middle Ages?	Change and Continuity	• What did the Industrial Revolution do for us?	Evidence	• Progress for all? Ordinary life around the world.	
Ordinary life – why did it change?	• Rats or rebels – which were the most significant?	Significance	• Why was ordinary life changing so much?	Evidence	• Government or technology? Why has life changed in twentieth century Britain?	Change and Continuity
Power, democracy and human rights	• Why did the barons rebel against King John? • Why were some kings deposed in the Middle Ages?	Causes and consequences	• Would you have signed Charles I's death warrant? • How did ordinary people win the right to vote?	Change and continuity Consequences	• Why do people let dictators take over? • Why is it important to remember the Holocaust? • Why did Black Americans have to fight so hard for civil rights?	Evidence Enquiry
Ideas and beliefs	• Henry VIII – medieval or modern?	Change and continuity	• What were they thinking about … ordinary life?	Evidence	• What can the Olympics tell us about the twentieth century?	Significance
Review	• What's been really important this year?	Significance	• What's been really important this year?	Significance	• Is JFK really so significant? • So what's been really important in KS3 History?	Significance

Overview of the Big Stories

The table below explains our approach to tackling the thematic stories identified in the Programme of Study. One important general point is that we have combined coverage of British, European and World histories into each thematic story because this creates a more coherent course for pupils, enabling them to compare and contrast developments in Britain and overseas.

Table 2: The approach to thematic stories

National Curriculum thematic stories	How we have tackled them across the series
Power The development of political power from the Middle Ages to the twentieth century, including changes in the relationship between rulers and the ruled over time, the changing relationship between the crown and parliament, and the development of democracy	We have treated this as two interconnected stories – the first being the story of monarchy (why monarchs were powerful and why royal power declined) and the second the story of the development of human rights which includes the French Revolution and the struggle for the vote in Britain, how rights can be lost and the consequences of this (e.g. in Nazi Germany) and finally struggles for equal rights, e.g. civil rights in the USA. These stories unfold across all three years.
The UK The different histories and changing relationships through time of the peoples of England, Ireland, Scotland and Wales	Examples illustrating this story appear in all three years of resources, as part of the other stories, particularly the stories of empire and conflict. But the overall story is tackled head on in Y8 with activities that can be found on the Year 8 Dynamic Learning CD to overview the whole story and activities to examine British identity and the identities of the four nations.
Movement and settlement The impact through time of the movement and settlement of diverse peoples to, from and within the British Isles	This story is introduced in Year 7 through family stories across time. The main focus is then on the story of emigration across time (in Year 8) and immigration across time (in Year 9). This enables pupils to compare answers to three core questions which apply to both emigration and immigration: • Why do people migrate? • How are they received? • What impacts do they have as migrants?
Ordinary life The way in which the lives, beliefs, ideas and attitudes of people in Britain have changed over time and the factors – such as technology, economic development, war, religion and culture – that have driven these changes	This story unfolds across all three years. The core is the story of ordinary life in Britain: firstly, describing the continuities and changes in core aspects – homes, work, health and leisure; secondly, investigating reasons why life has changed (including, for example, in Year 7 the Black Death and the revolt of 1381, and in Year 8 the impact of trade and industrialisation). Comparisons are drawn with other non-British societies.

Empire and trade The development of trade, colonisation, industrialisation and technology, the British Empire and its impact on different people in Britain and overseas, pre-colonial civilisations, the nature and effects of the slave trade, and resistance and decolonisation	We have focused this story squarely on empires, moving the sub-themes of industry and technology into the story of ordinary life. We provide short, focused, investigations on both the Roman (in Year 7) and Spanish (Year 8) Empires because it is misleading to study the British Empire alone. It was not the only empire in history and debates and controversies about the impact of empire do not relate to the British Empire alone. By tackling the same three core questions in relation to each empire, pupils will build up a broader sense of the history of empires. The Year 8 book includes a major enquiry on Thomas Clarkson and a discussion on his role in the abolition of slavery.
Conflict and co-operation The changing nature of conflict and co-operation between countries and peoples and its lasting impact on national, ethnic, racial, cultural or religious issues, including the nature and impact of the two world wars and the Holocaust, and the role of European and international institutions in resolving conflicts	We have developed this story across all three years focusing on attitudes to warfare, the effects of warfare and on significance: why some wars are remembered. We have focused on international co-operation in its widest sense, e.g. alliances against Fascism and international co-operation against hunger and natural disasters, rather than simply on organisations such as the League of Nations and the UN.
Ideas and beliefs The way in which the lives, beliefs, ideas and attitudes of people in Britain have changed over time	We have extracted this theme from the ordinary life story to give it more prominence and to give pupils more chance of understanding it. It forms part of the conclusion to each book, enabling pupils to identify the crucial changes in ideas, beliefs and attitudes in each period and how these help to link the thematic stories and explain many crucial developments.
Everything else! The impact of significant political, social, cultural, religious, technological and/or economic developments and events on past European and world societies	We have not treated this as a thematic story because it clearly isn't. We have embedded enquiries on developments and events within the thematic stories. For example, the story of India features in the stories of empire, and power and human rights.

Overview of concepts and processes

Each section of each book highlights one or two aspects of the concepts and processes. Clearly good history involves using them in combination, but for the purposes of defining enquiry questions and setting pupil activities we have focused on the concepts and processes that are germane to the line of investigation for each section.

Subsequent to each investigation the Doing History page pulls out and highlights for the pupil the key ideas about those concepts and processes that arise out of the work they have been doing. These are summarised in Table 3 below.

Table 3: Plan for concept and process progression through Years 7 to 9

Each enquiry/section is focused around one concept or process and the Doing History feature highlights, for the purposes of meta-cognition, the key ideas the pupils have confronted or used in that enquiry. The Doing History key ideas progress from year to year; each year introduces a more complex level of thinking about this concept or process which is in line with the National Curriculum statements of attainment. This table therefore summarises at a glance which aspects of each concept or process are distinctive or highlighted in each year. However it is important to note two points about this table and about Doing History progression in general:

- We separate the concepts and processes into rows to clarify progression, although in practice pupils use some concepts and processes together to pursue their enquiry – particularly in the later stages of the course.
- In practice the columns are not rigid either. Progression does not mean that you stop doing the thinking that characterised the previous year. Throughout this series there is a lot of reinforcement of a previous year's insights, and we revisit them to build on them.

Doing History	Year 7	Year 8	Year 9
Enquiry (and communication)	• asking questions • using sources to answer questions • explaining what happened but sometimes being uncertain • understanding the basic structure of essays and paragraphs and the importance of building a clear answer	• stages of enquiry, from asking questions to creating answers • asking questions linked to specific concepts • selecting sources that are relevant to a particular enquiry • developing skills in essay and paragraph writing and selecting precise words to create better written answers	• using a range of sources in order to reach reasoned conclusions • beginning to plan own enquiry, from asking questions to identifying relevant concepts to creating persuasive answers • being able to organise and communicate your ideas in a clear and convincing way
Chronological understanding	• putting people and events in the correct sequence in time • using the correct names for periods of history • being able to spot anachronisms	• developing a sense of period • identifying similarities and differences between periods • understanding diversity within periods • understanding the uses and the limitations of period labels	• being able to make links within and across different periods • building a chronological framework of periods that helps place new knowledge in its historical context

Sources	• sources are the clues that tell us about the past • sources are anything from the past (documents, artefacts, pictures, buildings, etc.)	• as we get nearer the present, more sources, and more types of sources, become available • having more sources allows you to find out more but makes the process of investigation more complex	• knowledge of the past is based on using as wide a range of sources as possible • knowledge of the past continues to develop as new sources used or discovered
Evidence	• identifying why sources don't always tell the whole truth • using a variety of sources • knowing how certain you are	• inferring from sources to look beyond the obvious • cross-referencing sources to establish support or contradiction • selecting sources in order to tell a particular story	• judging how useful a source is for your enquiry based on provenance/purpose and content/language of a source • judging how typical a source is – how much you can generalise from it • carefully selecting relevant information from a source to support an argument
Big Stories	• using Big Stories to see links between the people and events across time • using Big Stories to help understand what is happening today	• constructing your own Big Stories	• contesting Big Stories as interpretations
Diversity	• people's lives are different even if they live in the same period of history • people's lives are different even if they live in the same country in the same period of history	• making generalisations in order to sum up historical situations • it is important to test generalisations to make sure they are accurate	• diversity exists even within the stories of individuals • despite diversity the historian attempts to build valid generalisations about the past • able to make helpful generalisations and explain why others are misleading (e.g. myths)

Interpretations	• different people tell different stories about the past • they do this by including some people, topics or evidence and leaving out or down-playing others	• interpretations are determined by the attitude and beliefs of the person creating the interpretation • interpretations can be controversial	• interpretations can be controversial • interpretations can change because they reflect the circumstances in which they are made, the available evidence and the intentions of those who make them
Causes and consequences	• most events have a number of causes • even if there are a number of causes there's usually one that sets off an event – the trigger • causes are not usually equally important	• there are different types of causes and consequences • causes are often linked • events can have different consequences, such as short term and long term. They may also have unintended consequences – what happens may not be what people expected to happen	• causes are linked together – there is a cumulative effect; the same is true of consequences • looking for links can help to determine the importance of different causes and consequences • people argue about the main cause and consequence of an event; causes and consequences need prioritising by weighing the importance of one factor against another
Change and continuity	• at any one time, there are usually things that are changing and things that are staying the same • some changes happen quickly; some happen slowly	• a key change in a pattern of events is often called a turning-point – historians often study turning-points • things can get worse over time (regress) as well as getting better (progress)	• in order to assess the extent of a change you need a really good sense of the before and the after to make direct comparisons • change happens at a different pace in different parts of the world
Significance	• people use different criteria to decide what is significant and this leads to debates and arguments • being significant is not the same as being famous	• setting up criteria helps you make comparisons between different events • people disagree about what and who is significant – the choices they make reflect their own attitudes and values	• events can be significant because they tell us about ourselves and feed our sense of identity • statements about significance are contestable interpretations

Using this material in the classroom – lesson planning issues

Features of a Pupil's Book spread

Enquiry This book is full of enquiry questions to investigate. Some short enquiries will only take one lesson. Other longer ones – the depth studies – may spread over a number of weeks.

Quick History These are overviews that sum up long periods in a short activity.

Banner This introduces the enquiry and sums up what you are going to focus on.

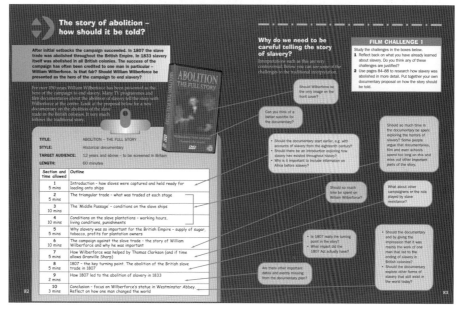

Activities These help you to build your enquiry step by step.

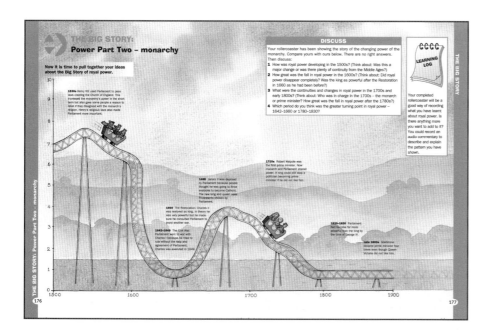

Big Story At the end of each section is a Big Story page that sums up the section and connects it with what has already been studied or with what is going to be studied. In this case, Power Part Two connects with Power Part One in the Year 7 book.

Themes Each section focuses on one thematic story. This section focuses on Power. You will probably have started this theme in Year 7 and will continue it in Year 9.

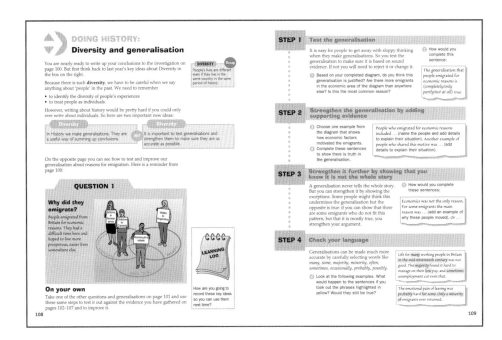

Doing History Each time you meet a new concept or process we recap the key ideas like this. If you want to get better at history this is what you focus on.

Learning Log This helps you to record what you have learned so you can use it next time.

How to... Step-by-step explanations of important history skills or writing skills that will help pupils to improve their work.

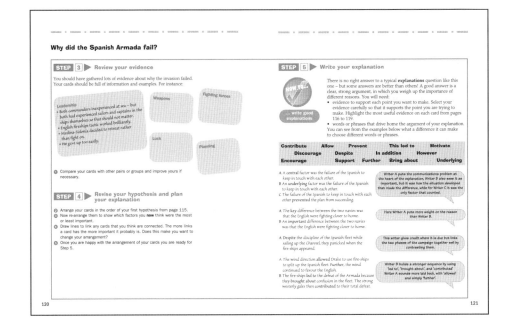

Features of Dynamic Learning

Dynamic Learning For every activity you will find on-screen activities and ICT-based investigations to help you.

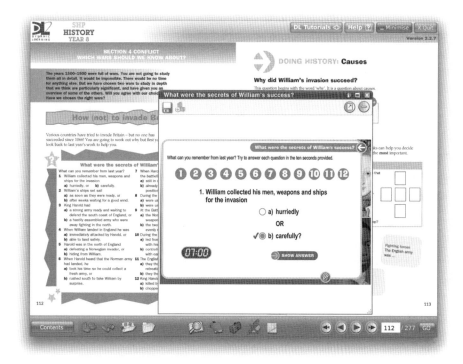

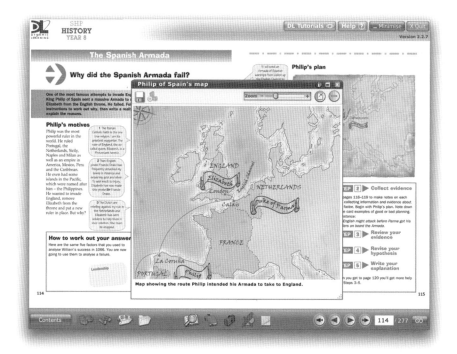

Text and images can be enlarged.

Pre-prepared lesson plans

The detailed notes on pages 27–95 provide lesson plans for all of Year 8. These are plans for 'lesson sequences' rather than for individual lessons. We have done this for a variety of reasons:

- lessons vary so much in length
- the first step towards building a coherent course for a year or for a whole key stage is to be able to build a coherent sequence of lessons
- most enquiries, to be worthwhile, carry over a number of lessons
- a lesson sequence gives you plenty of scope for choosing and adapting the material to suit your and your pupils' needs.

Each lesson sequence plan offers:

Summary	identifying enquiries, objectives and links to Big Stories
Approximate time required	but this depends on your choice of route
Key concepts and processes	links to the National Curriculum requirements
Resources	the major links to activities in the Pupil's Book, Dynamic Learning CD-ROM and TRB activity sheets
Objectives	expressed in terms of the knowledge and understandings pupils need to take forward to use later in KS3
Starter	ideas for starting the sequence with impact and clarity, to ensure pupils know what the following lessons are about
Development	how to use the Pupil's Book, CD and associated materials and activities to meet the lesson sequence objectives, with suggestions on alternative routes through the material
Plenary	how to ensure that the key points of the lesson sequence are recorded and understood by pupils, using the Big Story and Doing History activities and Learning Logs
Assessment for learning	indicators to look out for that identify successes or problems in learning
Other resources and linked activities	identifies optional resources, particularly on the CD

Each plan provides an outline. It is for you to make it your own as you choose which specific activities to use. There is much more in this book than you could easily fit into a one-year course. So it's not a case of simply doing everything in a section. Instead a number of options and short-cuts are built in to aid personalisation and differentiation – and to help you save time. These are explained in detail in the plans for each lesson sequence. For example, the suggestions on page 43 for a rapid treatment of the Spanish conquest of the Aztecs.

Customisable planning grid

You can also use the blank grid on the facing page for your own lesson sequence planning.

Lesson sequence plan	Enquiry title
Summary	
Number of lessons/time:	
Concepts and processes:	
Resources	
Objectives	
Starter	
Development	
Plenary	
Assessment for learning	

Dynamic Learning Lesson Builder

On the Dynamic Learning CD-ROM you will also find a Lesson Builder like this

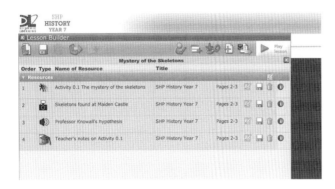

which allows you to mix together into a single lesson or lesson sequence any of
- the resources or activities from the Pupil's Book
- the Activity sheets on the CD in the back of this book
- the activities on the CD
- your own resources from your own VLE
- the web-based resources and investigations.

Planning backwards

If you are doing your own planning remember some basic principles. We have planned this course across the whole key stage. We have 'planned backwards' from an end point. We have identified what understandings we intend pupils to have by the end of KS3 History in terms of both
- the thematic stories, and
- the skills, processes and concepts.

These have defined our plan for each year and each lesson sequence within the year.
So begin by familiarising yourself with these Big Stories (see Table 2) and Doing History features (see Table 3). However you adapt the lesson sequences or create your own, bear these in mind, ensuring you are still able to reach a valid end point and an overall understanding. Work out your 'take away' then plan to achieve it.

Two-year KS3?

If you are delivering a two-year key stage then you have a particular need to focus on the essentials and ensure that all you do is important to your long-term objectives – what you want pupils to 'take away' from KS3. It is important not to dilute everything and try to

'cram it all in' more superficially; instead you need to focus your attention on the themes that you deem to be the core of KS3 yet still ensure that you cover all the concepts and processes. So from Table 1 you might decide to pursue only four of the six rows.

Here again the Dynamic Learning CD-ROM and its Lesson Builder will be a help. Once all three stages of this course are published and all three Dynamic Learning CDs available, you can freely mix together the ingredients from all three years to create your own lesson sequences.

Cross-curricular work – pros and cons

Cross-curricular work is again becoming fashionable (and indeed the planners of the KS3 review see it as the solution to all kinds of problems). But it is important to be aware (and make sure your management team is aware) that to be successful, every teacher involved needs to be thoroughly familiar with the nature of each subject being woven into the cross-curricular mix. Cross-curricular approaches will only work if teachers have a strong understanding of all the component disciplines and skills. It can be relatively easy to acquire the content knowledge to teach outside your specialism. But it can be somewhat harder to teach the processes and concepts of a new discipline, which are often finely nuanced. What a historian is looking for in handling source material is often very different from what the English department is looking for. Cross-curricular work must be balanced and must integrate the subjects effectively doing each one justice. This requires a significant investment in training and planning time, something which far too often is neglected. Even then bear in mind that cross-curricular approaches swim against the tide of teachers' own motivation and inclinations – and against pupils' and parents' expectations of what happens in schools. Pupils are almost always happier doing 'subjects' they recognise and to do otherwise puts standards of achievement in jeopardy.
The cross-curricular work that could promise some real value added is:
- Developing literacy skills and supporting extended writing. Much has already been written about this as part of the KS3 strategy. Literacy is strongly supported through this course, with many opportunities for the

development of reading, writing, speaking and listening skills, using classroom-tested strategies such as 'hamburger paragraphs' to help pupils understand what is required.

- Cross-curricular work with Citizenship. Citizenship is also naturally and deeply present in this course because of the emphasis on using knowledge and understanding of the past to inform our understanding of the present. Political literacy has been a shared concern for some time but a more recent opportunity is around 'identity'. Both subjects can contribute as equals to examinations of cultural or ethnic identity, and the importance of tolerance and recognising diversity.
- Activities based in the local area and environment with other Humanities departments in which the historical work can helpfully complement the work arising out of the objectives of your RE, Citizenship or Geography colleagues.

Differentiation and personalisation

We have ensured there is plenty of choice both in what pathway you take through this material and in how to tackle any given activity. We have also supported differentiation and personalisation in other ways:

- We encourage and value pupils asking their own questions – indeed the ability to ask your own questions and answer them is the holy grail of History teaching.
- Pupils are encouraged to make choices (in what they study and in how they record their findings).
- Activities are varied in difficulty and in learning style. Some are writing based; some are active; some can take place entirely in the computer suite. Different types of learners – visual, auditory or kinaesthetic – have opportunities to succeed and to show what they can do.
- Pupils are often asked to work in pairs or groups to do activities. You can structure the groups so that lower ability pupils work alongside more able pupils or, when the tasks vary, put pupils in same ability groups.
- Interactive tasks allow the pupils to demonstrate their ideas to each other so pupils can learn from each other.
- Answers are modelled or opportunities are provided for teachers to model activities with the class, so pupils can see how to improve their performance.

- More difficult activities are scaffolded to support lower attainers, e.g. pupils may be given a writing frame to structure their response. More able pupils can be encouraged to do without these aids.
- Many activities provide more challenge for higher ability pupils. They develop ideas related to the main activities, often based on the sort of questions that more able pupils themselves tend to ask.
- The big tasks are open ended and are intended as an opportunity for all pupils to show what they can do – not just the higher ability pupils. They allow differentiation by outcome.
- Lesson sequence plans in the Teacher's Resource Book suggest many ways in which lessons can be differentiated. Specifically, they suggest forms of support and extension for lower and higher ability pupils.

Managing active learning

We have included a number of kinaesthetic activities. We have been trialling these widely over the past few years and seen how well they can motivate learning and how effectively they help pupils build big pictures on which they can hang later learning. We are very keen that all pupils have the opportunity to try these out. However, in managing such activities always think carefully in advance about the nature of the individual class, the space you have available and whether kinaesthetic activity suits the class, the time of day, what they have done in previous lessons and other variables. Never assume because an activity worked last year or with another class it will necessarily work with all classes.

To help class management, in the activities associated with this series unnecessary and uncontrolled movement is cut out, keeping movement by pupils under your direction. This enables you to focus on pupils' thinking, their questions and your own questions to develop their understanding. In more complex kinaesthetic activities, such as the factors bringing about the Industrial Revolution (Pupil's Book page 25), there are ways to simplify the activity so there is more or less moving about to meet your management needs. For more information about the principles and management of active learning and for kinaesthetic versions of more of the activities in the books and CDs in this series, see **www.thinkinghistory.co.uk**.

Creating Learning Logs

The Learning Logs (in the Pupil's Book, CD and TRB) are a key element in this course, regularly prompting pupils to record what they have found out, and so to help them build up their understandings in a coherent and progressive way across KS3.

This applies particularly to:

- Big Stories – pupils use Learning Logs to record key points in the development of each thematic story (e.g. Ordinary life) so that by the end of KS3 they have an overview of its development and can re-tell the essential features
- Doing History – pupils record each new key idea and exemplify it from the work they have completed.

We have offered various ways of recording findings: mind maps, diagrams, podcasts, PowerPoints, etc. Using the CD you can use the Post It note feature or the Toolbox. Post It notes can be created at any time and pasted on that spread and saved, so they will be there next time you come back to that spread and can be added to at any time. They can be exported to a Word document. In the same way the Dynamic Learning toolbox can be used to draw diagrams, or pictures or graffiti that can be saved as a screen shot for later use.

However, Learning Logs are supposed to be personal. The important thing is that pupils make the Learning Log their own. Whatever medium we have suggested, if you have a better one or are used to doing it a different way please adapt accordingly.

Familiarise yourself with the Dynamic Learning disc

Think of the Pupil's Book, this Teacher's Resource Book and the forthcoming Dynamic Learning disc as parts of a whole. The three components taken together give you massively greater flexibility to adapt to the learning needs of your students than if you had only the Pupil's Book.

The SHP History Year 8 Dynamic Learning disc is available from autumn 2009 so this is a preview of its features and functionality. There is also a demo available to download at **www.hoddereducation.co.uk/shphistory**. Dynamic Learning helps you in your teaching in three main ways.

1 It makes it easier to find and use each individual feature of the Pupil Book
The Dynamic Learning disc gives you all the pages of the Pupil's Book. Each feature of the page is openable in a pop-up for you to zoom in or annotate (see page 17). All the author text, the written sources, the pictures, the diagrams, the tasks – all can be launched on your whiteboard, saved to your network or exported to become part of your own personalised lesson. All the worksheets from this Teacher's Resource Book can also be found on the Dynamic Learning disc.

2 It makes it easier to build your own lessons and load them to your VLE

The Lesson Builder, which is incorporated into Dynamic Learning, makes it even easier to design and deliver creative lessons using the textbook resources. You simply drag and drop resources from the textbook into your lesson, combine them with your own resources, or resources from the internet, and then save them with a single click for your VLE (NB this will work with any VLE) for colleagues to share, or for pupils to use at home or at school.

3 It is full of additional activities and resources

Dynamic Learning additional activities fall into two categories:

- Some activities are simple five-minute tasks to fit into a lesson, for example as a starter, or a review/plenary. We call these 'mini' activities.
- Others are much more sustained digitally based lessons or lesson sequences where all the learning could take place using computers. We call these 'maxi' activities (see example, right). The maxi activities largely use Office-based applications such as PowerPoint, Word, Excel or creative applications such as MovieMaker.

Sometimes these additional activities provide new ways of tackling the tasks that are in the Pupil's Book: one way in the Pupil's Book; another in Dynamic Learning. For example, the large pictures on pages 4–11 are available in Dynamic Learning with 'hot spots' plus questions for pupils to explore in class or on their own. Sometimes the activities are brand new – covering topics or ideas that were hard to tackle in the confines of a textbook or which work better in the electronic medium – e.g. decision-making exercises; animated accounts of the six Big Stories; make your own movies; animations. Finally, some provide specialised additional content (e.g. the story of the changing relationship between England, Ireland, Scotland and Wales).

We also provide audio versions of important written sources.

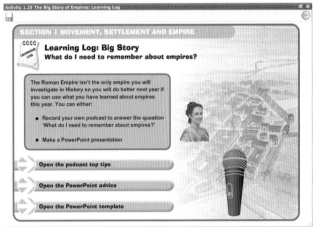

Joined-up planning

Variety of approach is clearly important in maintaining pupils' interest and motivation but this whole set of resources has been put together to help you plan coherently without sacrificing varied learning styles. The choice of which to use and how to mix the Pupil's Book, the worksheets and Dynamic Learning has got to be determined by the nature of each class, the context of each lesson and the learning needs of the pupils – and that's where your professional judgement will make the best of the variety of resources on offer.

⇄) Assessment

The new KS3 National Curriculum includes new level descriptions for Levels 4–8 (see opposite). Levels 1–3 were seen as most relevant to KS1 and KS2, which are covered by the current review. The revised levels should look broadly familiar to you. The intention of the re-written descriptions is two-fold:

- to make the distinctions between levels clearer
- to show that the different strands running through the levels are inter-dependent and should not be separated. Progress in one depends on, and assists progress in another.

Summative assessment

National Curriculum assessment in History still requires teachers to reach a judgement about each Pupil's work, based on the evidence of what pupils do as they progress through their KS3 course. Teachers look for the 'best fit' between the level descriptors and the work that the pupil has produced. The way in which this assessment is carried out in practice will depend on specific school assessment policies and how History departments interpret them. However, the two most common approaches are:

- to survey all the work a pupil has done over a period (say, half a year)
- to set specific tasks (say, four to six a year) targeted on part of the level descriptors which are the culmination of work done over some time.

There is little need to revisit your current assessment policy if it is working to everyone's satisfaction.

This series provides many opportunities for teachers to carry out their summative judgements about the National Curriculum level reached by their pupils. Table 1 on page 9 and the lesson sequence plans show which concepts and processes form the focus for each section and lesson sequence. Each lesson sequence includes pieces of work (including written work, oral work, diagrams, PowerPoints) that contribute evidence of attainment.

Formative assessment

Good practice in Assessment for Learning is also well-embedded in most History departments. Teachers are well versed in the need to share objectives, to model answers, to give precise feedback, to use self-assessment and peer assessment, as well as in the different approaches to marking pupils' work. To help you do this each lesson sequence has:

- a clear and overt concept or process objective
- a set of tasks which build towards this objective – carefully planned and with outcomes modelled where appropriate
- plenty of opportunity for group work and discussion about, for example, what makes a good question
- advice on the kinds of indicators to look out for that identify successes or problems in learning.

The most obvious new opportunities for formative assessment provided in this course are the Learning Logs and the predictive activities.

- On the Dynamic Learning CD-ROM each section of the Introduction (1750, 1850, 1900) begins with an on-screen activity called 'How much change?' Similarly, in the Big Graph Challenge (Section 1), pupils predict the shape of the standard of living graph for the forthcoming period. They save it and return to it at any stage through the section to see how their ideas are developing.
- Each Big Story and each Doing History concludes with a Learning Log. Pupils record their learning so far. This is their own record, but it will reveal a level of understanding and engagement that can form a clear basis for constructive feedback.

Neither of these features is intended solely for assessment purposes but they do provide a clear picture of a pupil's current skills and level of understanding and allow you to tailor your feedback more appropriately.

Level 4

Pupils show their knowledge and understanding of local, national and international history by describing some of the main events, people and periods they have studied, and by identifying where these fit within a chronological framework. They describe characteristic features of past societies and periods to identify change and continuity within and across different periods and to identify some causes and consequences of the main events and changes. They identify and describe different ways in which the past has been interpreted. When finding answers to historical questions, they begin to use information as evidence to test hypotheses. They begin to produce structured work, making appropriate use of dates and terms.

Level 5

Pupils show their knowledge and understanding of local, national and international history by describing events, people and some features of past societies and periods in the context of their developing chronological framework. They begin to recognise and describe the nature and extent of diversity, change and continuity, and to suggest relationships between causes. They suggest some reasons for different interpretations of the past and they begin to recognise why some events, people and changes might be judged as more historically significant than others. They investigate historical problems and issues and begin to ask their own questions. They begin to evaluate sources to establish evidence for particular enquiries. They select and deploy information and make appropriate use of historical terminology to support and structure their work.

Level 6

Pupils show their knowledge and understanding of local, national and international history by beginning to analyse the nature and extent of diversity, change and continuity within and across different periods. They begin to explain relationships between causes. They begin to explain how and why different interpretations of the past

have arisen or been constructed. They explore criteria for making judgements about the historical significance of events, people and changes. They investigate historical problems and issues, asking and beginning to refine their own questions. They evaluate sources to establish relevant evidence for particular enquiries. They select, organise and deploy relevant information and make appropriate use of historical terminology to produce structured work.

Level 7

Pupils show their knowledge and understanding of local, national and international history by analysing historical change and continuity, diversity and causation. They explain how and why different interpretations of the past have arisen or been constructed. They begin to explain how the significance of events, people and changes has varied according to different perspectives. They investigate historical problems and issues, asking and refining their own questions and beginning to reflect on the process undertaken. When establishing the evidence for a particular enquiry, pupils consider critically issues surrounding the origin, nature and purpose of sources. They select, organise and use relevant information and make appropriate use of historical terminology to produce well-structured work.

Level 8

Pupils show their knowledge and understanding of local, national and international history by constructing substantiated analyses about historical change and continuity, diversity and causation. They analyse and explain a range of historical interpretations and different judgements about historical significance. They suggest lines of enquiry into historical problems and issues, refining their methods of investigation. They evaluate critically a range of sources and reach substantiated conclusions independently. They use historical terminology confidently, reflecting on the way in which terms can change meaning according to context. They produce precise and coherent work.

Exceptional performance

Pupils show a confident and extensive knowledge and understanding of local, national and international history. They use this to frame and pursue enquiries about historical change and continuity, diversity and causation, constructing well-substantiated, analytic arguments within a wide frame of historical reference. They analyse links between events and developments that took place in different countries and in different periods. When exploring historical interpretations and judgements about significance, pupils construct convincing and substantiated arguments and evaluations based on their understanding of the historical context. They evaluate critically a wide range of sources, reaching substantiated conclusions independently. They use historical terminology confidently, reflectively and critically. They consistently produce precise and coherent narratives, descriptions and explanations.

INTRODUCTION OVERVIEW

The introduction is designed to provide a brief overview of the chronology of this book (1500–1900) and introduces some of the key features of this period of history.

⮁⟩ Lesson sequence 1: The book with no name (pp. 2–13)

A rapid overview of how Britain looked at four points in the book's chronology: 1500, 1750, 1850 and 1900. Pupils look for similarities and differences, changes and continuities across time.

⏩ **Plan for lesson sequence 1**	# The book with no name

Summary	This enquiry provides a broad overview of the chronological span of this book. It is intended to be taken rapidly, with plenty of questions, discussion and reminders of earlier periods and their key features.
Time needed	1 hour
Key concepts and processes	**Enquiry:** asking questions; generating hypotheses **Chronology:** understanding and using dates, as well as the correct vocabulary and conventions for describing periods and the passing of time; beginning to develop a sense of period and a sense of the characteristic features of different periods; beginning to build a chronological framework **Change and continuity:** beginning to identify and analyse changes and continuities within and between periods
Resources	• Pupil's Book pages 2–13 • Activity sheets 1 and 2

⏩ Objectives

By the end of this enquiry pupils should know about or understand:
- some key features of history 1500–1900
- some of the changes and continuities of those years
- some of the similarities and differences between the periods covered by those four hundred years
- that people's lives and the environment changed, sometimes slowly, sometimes quickly
- that labelling periods is helpful, but poses problems.

⏩ Lesson sequence

Starter

The essence of this unit is speed: a rapid 'fly-thru' of four hundred years using visual images.
- Have the four scenes from pages 4–11 playing on the whiteboard as pupils arrive, to arouse curiosity.
- Start with the familiar: use the images from page 3 to remind pupils of previous work on

the Middle Ages. Draw their attention to the possible titles for that period. Ask for choices and brief arguments to defend each choice.
- Introduce the challenge – 'The book with no name': they must try to come to a consensus about what this period 1500–1900 is.

Development

The intention is for pupils to paint a broad-brush picture of the four centuries they are going to be studying this year, using the four picture spreads on pages 4–11. It is not to analyse and explain each one in detail – they will be spending time on that later.

Step 1

Divide the class into six groups, each taking responsibility for one question across time:
1. What kind of work did people do?
2. What were their homes like?
3. What was their religion?
4. Who was their ruler?
5. Could they lead healthy lives?
6. What was the quality of their environment?

Begin by focusing on pages 4–5 (the year 1500), and ask each group to find the answer to their question and report back, completing the CD screen grid or Activity sheet 1. Remind them that 1500 is the date they had reached at the end of last year, so they should know some of the answers.

Differentiation note: questions 5 and 6 are harder, requiring some inference skills beyond straight comprehension. (Use these GCSE words *inference* and *comprehension* whenever you can.)

Step 2

Set groups free to find the answers to their question on the other three spreads, again collecting answers on the CD screen grid or Activity sheet 1.

Step 3

Build up an overview of each of the different dates from the answers that have been collected. Award marks out of 10 for the amount of change between each date, with10 equalling 'everything changed'.

1750: At this point, there is apparently more continuity than change from 1500, even though 250 years have passed. Encourage pupils to look for small signs of change.

1850: As the pupils discover dramatic change, introduce the idea of *progress*. Is change always good?

1900: Too often pupils are left in 1850, in early Industrial Britain. But the period from 1850 to the outbreak of the First World War was, in many important ways, very different and with some progress in many fields.

(Use the words *change* and *continuity* while commenting on what groups have discovered.)

Plenary

Use pages 12–13 – Doing History: Chronology – as the concluding activity. Questions 1–4 are for quick discussion, but questions 5 and 6 use Activity sheet 2 to introduce some events and people from this period. This sheet will also serve as a handy reference as pupils work through the five main sections of the book. Chronology is best developed in short, frequent doses, not worked on at great length. Refer to dates, before and after, continually as you teach, particularly when introducing new topics or people.

⬍⟩ Assessment for Learning – Outcomes to look for

a) Can pupils remember period names from KS2 and Year 7?
b) Can they put a date into the correct century?
c) Can pupils recognise differences between the medieval period and this one?
d) Can pupils recognise differences between earlier and later centuries in the period 1500–1900?

SECTION 1 OVERVIEW
ORDINARY LIFE: WHAT DID THE INDUSTRIAL REVOLUTION DO FOR US?

In this section pupils investigate ordinary lives in the three periods into which the years 1500–1900 were divided in the introduction.

Traditionally, teaching was concentrated on the key event of this period, the Industrial Revolution, which lies at the heart of this book. Study of the preceding years was mainly political history and the years after 1850 were also largely ignored. This National Curriculum requires a more thematic treatment. The enquiries are explicit about new sources of evidence for the lives of ordinary people. The concept of progress underlies all the lesson sequences.

◆） Lesson sequence 2: Ordinary lives 1500–1750 (pp. 14–23)

The main challenge for the whole section is set up. Pupils work on a new type of evidence and take part in a game following three families through these years.

◆） Lesson sequence 3: What did the Industrial Revolution do for us? (pp. 24–31)

The Industrial Revolution affected every aspect of life in Britain, but the focus here is on how it changed people's lives. Pupils also find out about more new kinds of evidence.

◆） Lesson sequence 4: A better time for all? Ordinary life 1850–1900 (pp. 32–49)

This sequence starts by investigating ordinary lives through the evidence of Victorian photographs. It concludes by pulling together the patterns of the lives of ordinary people 1500–1900, including their ideas and beliefs.

⟫ Plan for lesson sequence 2	# Ordinary lives 1500–1750
Summary	The main challenge for the whole section is set up on page 15. It establishes links with work done in the previous year, and will lead on to enquiries in Year 9. Pupils then make inferences using a new kind of source which has been made available to us only since the sixteenth century – inventories – to ask the question: 'Which home would you like to live in?' *Roll up! Roll up! Take a chance on life!* is a game which makes clear that 'ordinary lives' are not all the same, and differences of wealth, as well as chance factors, affect what happens to families.
Time needed	2 hours
Key concepts and processes	**Evidence:** inference from inventories **Change and continuity** linked to the idea of progress/regress **Diversity** of people's lives and experiences in the past
Resources	• Pupil's Book pages 14–23 • Activity sheets 3–6

⟫ Objectives

By the end of this enquiry pupils should be able to:
• understand that people's lives in the past were diverse, affected by wealth, region, religion, gender
• understand that national political, religious or economic events had social implications for ordinary lives
• recognise that chance plays a big part in how family life changes over time
• make judgements about what progress is and how to assess it.

⟫ Lesson sequence

Starter

• If your class used the Year 7 book in this series, remind them of, or ask them to bring in, the work they did on 'The Big Story graph' (page 188–89 in the Year 7 book). Discuss what changes took place in the Middle Ages and what might happen from 1500 to the present.

• If you didn't use the Year 7 book, go straight to the graph on pages 14–15. Refer to the Quick History on pages 4–11. Discuss what the four pictures suggest for the course of the graph between 1500 and 1900.
• Use Activity sheet 3 to plot a graph for 1500–1750.

Development

The inventory activity, pages 16–17, both introduces a new type of source and begins to increase awareness of diversity. As the National Curriculum states: 'Diversity exists within and between groups.'
Explain what an inventory is. Can pupils compile an inventory of their bedroom, from memory? If they swap inventories, what does the list tell their partner about them? This activity has good scope for differentiation: matching inventory to family is quite easy, but the inference questions (2 and 4) need some thought.
Further questioning could bring out the slow improvements in standard of living through this period.

Pupils can record their answers on Activity Sheet 4.

For the 'Roll up! Roll up!' game on pages 18–21, put the class into groups of three: each person represents one of the families. Some pupils will try to rush through this, wanting to finish and see who's 'won'. Encourage them to slow down, to read the alternatives, to see what other courses they might have been made to follow. Use Activity Sheet 5 to record answers. The important lessons here are in the de-briefing, of course. Some topics to discuss, apart from those listed in the Activity box on page 21, are:

- further experiences of diversity. The National Curriculum refers to '… social, economic, political and religious differences' as well as what are probably the more expected 'cultural, ethnic, linguistic' differences. Awareness of diversity of several kinds strengthens the concept
- some of the big events of this period, but at this point introduce them 'from the bottom up'. Don't try to go into detail about any of these events – that will come later. This activity is about the personal impact of national events
- the importance of chance.

The first stopping point on the Big Graph Challenge comes on pages 22–23. Sources 1 and 2 on page 22 serve as a reminder of what pupils learned in Year 7, and provide a pattern for the story so far. In Year 7, pupils should have noted that: 'At any one time, there are usually things that are changing and things that are not.'

There are two questions in the activity on page 23: question 1 involves summarising what they have found out from the introduction, the inventories and the game. Pupils work in pairs and use Activity sheet 6 to complete the final column of the table, in pairs. Their responses

can then be collated on a class table, using the whiteboard. Note the extra information on page 22 on population and percentage living in towns. The figure of one in five Britons already living in towns or cities was far higher than any other country and prepared Britain for the industrialisation soon to happen.

Plenary

Use Activity sheets 3–6 to then complete question 2 of the activity: draw the graph of progress, based on the class views expressed in the table. Class suggestions for Post-It notes to explain what factors affected people's lives will draw on the factors covered in the whole enquiry.

◆ Assessment for Learning – Outcomes to look for

a) Can pupils recognise differences between their own lives and the lives of people in the past?
b) Can they recognise differences between the lives of people at two different times in the past?
c) Can they recognise differences between different groups of people living at the same time in the past?
d) Can pupils identify both changes and continuities over time?
e) Can pupils make judgements about issues of progress and regress?
f) Can pupils work together effectively and express advantages in working in this way?

Linked web-based activities

The Big Story of Everyday Life
http://www.thinkinghistory.co.uk/ActivityBase /BigStoryEverydayLife.html

Plan for lesson sequence 3	**What did the Industrial Revolution do for us? 1750–1850**
Summary	The Industrial Revolution is sometimes taught as if it was about machines, or capital, but this enquiry focuses on the impact on people's lives. The main activity is a source investigation of people in Manchester, their work, homes and quality of life. It also introduces some new sources.
Time needed	2 hours
Key concepts and processes	**Evidence:** comprehension, inference and synthesis of sources; evaluation of utility for purpose **Cause and consequence:** multiple causes and how they are linked **Change and continuity:** Rapid and profound change
Resources	• Pupil's Book pages 24–31 • Activity sheets 7A and 7B, 8–10

Objectives

By the end of this enquiry pupils should be able to:
• understand some of the ways the Industrial Revolution changed Britain
• explain the factors which caused it, and how they are linked
• understand how people's lives changed.

Lesson sequence

Starter

Start with the pictures on page 30 (see also Activity sheet 9). Both are about making iron, but Source 1 is before the Industrial Revolution and Source 2 is after. Ask the class about the changes: Where is this happening? Who is working? How many people are working? What machines are being used?

Then refer to the 'Before and after' table on page 24. Emphasise that this is by far the biggest change in the history they will study this year. Use Activity sheet 7A to add more changes as you work through the rest of this section (pages 24–49).

Development

• You should explain the nine causal factors of the Industrial Revolution (page 25), before pupils do the activity on page 24. Activity sheet 7B can be used for question 2. Use words like *cause*, *factor*, and *links* to build up an understanding of this concept. Put together a whole-class version of the activity, looking for as many – properly explained – links as possible.

• The four-page enquiry on the impact of industrialisation on people's lives in Manchester (pages 26–29) can either be tackled quite slowly, with every pupil working through each of the twelve sources, or much more quickly by dividing up the class and sources: two sources to each of six groups. The pupils need to try to find answers to the three big questions a)–c) in the activity on page 26. Activity sheet 8 can be used to record answers.

• Move to questions 1–4 in the activity on page 26 when the whole class has reported back and each pupil is familiar with all twelve of the sources. Be sure to use the term 'evaluate' here. You could introduce the idea, and the term, *reliability*, drawing attention to the different kinds of sources, for example statistics, paintings, reports, etc.

Plenary

Use Activity sheets 10 and then 3 to continue
the 'Big Graph Challenge' (pages 30–31),
based on the class views expressed in the table.
Compare with the graph plotted for 1500–1750.

◆〉 Assessment for Learning – Outcomes to look for

a) Can pupils explain one cause of
   industrialisation?
b) Can they explain several?
c) Can they link causes together?
d) Can pupils identify changes to people's lives?
e) Can they make a judgement about whether
   the changes were progress or not?

Linked web-based activities

The Big Story of Everyday Life
**http://www.thinkinghistory.co.uk/ActivityBase
/BigStoryEverydayLife.html**

A better time for all?
Ordinary life 1850–1900

Summary	This section concludes with an enquiry into, first, the impact of railways on Victorian Britain, then several other aspects of life in this important later industrial phase. The activities pull together the important ideas in this section – evidence, change and continuity. We finish with an investigation of how ideas and beliefs, as well as material conditions, changed over the four hundred years of this book.
Time needed	3–4 hours, or more if the display activity is developed.
Key concepts and processes	**Evidence:** comprehension; inference; cross-referencing; utility **Change and continuity:** over short and very long periods **Communication:** an ability to present knowledge and understanding in a variety of ways
Resources	• Pupil's Book pages 32–49 • Activity Sheets 11–15

➤ Objectives

By the end of this enquiry pupils should be able to:
• understand the continuing changes taking place in Britain in the second half of the nineteenth century and the impact of these on people's lives
• work with a wide range of sources and draw some general conclusions from them
• select and deploy information in order to communicate understanding of historical processes
• understand the factors that caused specific changes
• understand that values and beliefs changed as well as more tangible aspects of life.

➤ Lesson sequence

Starter

Ask the students to look at – or put up on the whiteboard – Source 3 on page 22 and Source 6 on page 33. In what ways are these two photographs evidence of the impact of the railways in late nineteenth century Britain? Go on to compare Sources 1 and 2 on page 32. Why are they so different?

Development

• Complete the activity on page 32: the questions deal with change, continuity and progress.
• Play the set of photographs from pages 34–39 on the whiteboard. Look for impressions of change, of progress. Ask pupils just to talk about what they see, and what the photo might mean for people's lives in Britain. Only then move to the more formal activity on page 34. Use Activity sheet 11 to record answers.

Or, to get pupils to really look at the pictures, project Source 1 from page 34 with most of the picture blanked out – keep just one person. Ask the class what they think the photo shows. Gradually reveal more of the photo, questioning tightly each time.
You may be able to add more photographs from your local area to include in the display.

Other results of the railway expansion:
○ All clocks in Britain had to keep the same time. Before the railways, local time was kept: Bristol, for example, was six minutes ahead of London.
○ National newspapers began.
○ National Trade Unions became possible.

- o Fresh milk could be delivered into towns direct from the countryside. Before this, cows were kept in many cities.
  - o Jobs: by 1850 there were 50,000 people working on the railways.
  - o Bridges, cuttings, viaducts and embankments changed the look of rural Britain.
  - o New towns grew up just to service railways: Crewe, Doncaster, Wolverton, Swindon.
- The Doing History activity on page 40 requires pupils to practise all the skills of using evidence which they have learned about in this section: not only *comprehension* but *inference, cross-referencing, selection* and, for some, *utility* and *reliability*. Use these terms as you prepare pupils for bullet points 3 and 4 of the task. Draw their attention to the Language Boxes for Inference, Cross-referencing and Selection. Encourage them to use the terms and the words in the Language Boxes in the explanations which accompany their choice.
  More evidence, including local sources, could be introduced here.
  Use Activity sheet 14 to complete the Learning Log.
- The last part of the Big Graph Challenge is prepared over pages 42–45. The subjectivity of any judgement is made overt by bringing me, the author, into the story: it is clear that this is an interpretation. Hopefully, different interpretations have been emerging in the class, too.
- The 'baskets' activity on page 45 adds in yet more information about the period 1850–1900: use Activity sheet 13 to complete it (this should be worked through quickly).
- Finish the Change and Continuity story by completing the Big Graph Challenge using Activity sheet 3. Then use Activity sheet 14 to record the Learning Log on this key concept.
- Each section of this book includes activities which examine changes in what the National Curriculum lists as 'beliefs, ideas and attitudes' over the period. This section has been mainly about practical, material changes. Now is the time for pupils to overview changes in the beliefs, ideas and attitudes of ordinary people, recalling those of the Tudor period and pairing them with

those from late Victorian Britain. Pupils will have picked up enough from this section to complete the six blank thought bubbles on page 49, although they may need to look back over the section to remind themselves. Use Activity sheet 15 as a card-sort exercise; pupils can record answers on the blank cards. Again, a follow-up discussion could look at changes and continuities.

Plenary

Use the completed Big Graph to overview this section. What were the turning-points? When did life get better? If doing this on a whiteboard from the CD, add Post-It notes to help explain the shape of the graph.
Alternatively, use the activity on ideas and beliefs described above as the plenary.

⇕⟩ Assessment for Learning – Outcomes to look for

a) Can pupils demonstrate the ability to comprehend and infer from sources?
b) Can they cross-refer sources to make an account or explanation?
c) Can they select sources to support their argument?
d) Can pupils recognise changes, and evaluate their impact?
e) Can they recognise continuity over a period?
f) Can they compare past situations with the present?
g) Can they compare two different past situations?
h) Can pupils communicate their thoughts, descriptions, explanations and arguments effectively, structuring them and using dates and historical terms appropriately?

Linked web-based activities

The Big Story of Everyday Life
http://www.thinkinghistory.co.uk/ActivityBase/BigStoryEverydayLife.html
Physical version of pages 44–45: factors linked to big graph
http://www.thinkinghistory.co.uk/ActivityBase/EverydayLifeFactors.html

SECTION 2 OVERVIEW
EMPIRE: WHY WERE EUROPEANS MAD ABOUT EMPIRES?

This section builds on the thematic story of Empire, started in Year 7, and includes the compulsory topic of the slave trade. The key concepts of Cause and consequence and Interpretations are developed from prior learning and pupils are given the opportunity to improve their Enquiry skills.

◆〉 Lesson sequence 5: The Spanish Empire (pp. 50–65)

How did the Spaniards come to have an empire in America and what impact did this empire have on the Native Americans? Pupils make links with their knowledge of the Romans and the key questions that were introduced in Year 7.

◆〉 Lesson sequence 6: The British Empire and the slave trade (pp. 66–89)

An enquiry into the slave trade and the story of abolition giving pupils the opportunity to evaluate evidence and present their findings orally.

◆〉 Lesson sequence 7: The British Empire (pp. 90–97)

This is a brief overview of the story of the British Empire, focusing on possible different interpretations.

The Spanish Empire

Summary	The British Empire is a compulsory element in the new, 2008, KS3 History curriculum but it is important that pupils do not think it was the only empire. This sequence of lessons makes links back to the story of empires in the Year 7 book by using the same key questions. It focuses on the development of the Spanish Empire, looking at the motives and attitudes of the conquistadors and the winners and losers in their conquest. Finally, 'Doing History' looks at Interpretations, highlighting the need for caution in telling the stories of empire.
Time needed	3–4 hours
Key concepts and processes	**Cause and consequence:** the Spanish conquest of Mexico **Interpretations:** of empires **Using Evidence:** the Aztec way of life
Resources	• Pupil's Book pages 50–65 • Activity sheets 16–20

→ Objectives

By the end of this enquiry pupils should:
- be able to use accurately and explain the terms empire, colony, colonist, 'mother country', conquest
- understand, be able to exemplify and be starting to make links between motives for acquiring empires
- understand and be able to exemplify various positive and negative effects that being part of an empire has on those involved
- be able to identify factors that empire builders have in common
- recognise that an interpretation of an historical event is determined by the attitudes and beliefs of the person creating it and therefore interpretations can be controversial.

⇕ Lesson sequence

Starter

The detail and colour in the picture on pages 50–51 provide a 'hook' with which all pupils can engage but, although there is potential for prolonged discussion, this should not take more than about 10 minutes. Questioning should focus on comparisons and inference.

Discuss:
- the strength of the Spanish conquistadors, in their armour, weapons and horses
- the strength and culture of the Aztecs. They clearly have wealth, building skills, culture and a hierarchical organisation. To defend themselves they have numerical superiority but, despite the gold adornments, do not have steel to use for protection or sophisticated weapons, which should be noted, as it becomes relevant in a later activity
- the picture suggests the Spanish will benefit greatly from Aztec riches but also that they expect to be the salvation of the Aztec people because they are bringing Christianity, indicated by the crucifix
- it would be worth including the nineteenth century origin of the painting in the discussion and asking if a modern artist is likely to have the same attitude.

It is important to keep making connections with prior learning – the final activity question on page 50 asks for speculation on the outcome of the meeting, based on any previous knowledge of empires, most probably what happened in Britain when the Romans arrived. Draw attention to the three key questions in the Big Story of Empire (page 51) before moving on.

Development

The information and activities on pages 52–59 are about the reasons for the Spanish conquest of the Aztecs. This can be done individually, in pairs or as group work.

A quick history of European empires (pages 52–53)
Before allowing pupils to complete the map activity it is worth checking their understanding of terminology and basic geography! Activity sheet 16 will help in completing the task but it may be useful to create the headline for 1600 with the whole class as a model for the other three; for example: *Spain and Portugal lead the world by setting up new empires*.
Pupils should use the information boxes on the maps and prior knowledge to come up with reasons for Europeans wanting empires but this task is not intended to be more than a quick summary to provide background.

Travellers' tales: how would the Spaniards describe the Aztecs? (pages 54–59)
The main activity in this lesson sequence needs no further explanation. However, if time allocation is a problem the class could be divided into groups of three, one looking at war, one at wealth and one at religion, with the three coming together to share ideas and produce a combined report. This report would then be reviewed by swapping with another group and discussing the questions. Activity sheet 17 can be used for the key points in the final report. Pupils may need to be reminded that they are looking at the Aztecs from the point of view of the Spanish Cortes and not as twenty-first century school pupils.

How did the Spanish defeat of the Aztecs change Spain and Mexico? (pages 60–61)
Activity questions 1–2: Any features in the painting (Source 2) that show the power, wealth, skills, culture or creativity of the Aztecs are acceptable for the list.
Questions 3–5: In listing winners and losers, the Spanish clearly 'won' and the Aztecs 'lost', but pupils need to identify the different groups of Spaniards who benefited, both initially and later on. Answers could easily be combined to record in a chart:

Winners	Ways in which they won
Spain, the 'mother country'	imposed its laws and culture on Mexico; increased its power and influence in the world
Cortes' followers	became major landowners
Spanish colonists	used Mexico as a starting point to gain new lands, e.g. Pizarro in Peru
Roman Catholic Church	spread its influence and teaching to the Americas
City of Seville	gained great wealth, which led to new buildings, including the magnificent cathedral
Losers	**Ways in which they lost**
Moctezuma and his people	destruction of Tenochtitlan; end of Aztec Empire
Native Americans in much of the Spanish Empire	many wiped out by disease; culture and heritage virtually destroyed; end of freedom and prosperity
Black Africans	became part of slave trade to Americas

The Big Story: Empire Part Two (pages 62–63)
The Big Story returns to the three key questions to summarise the main learning points about empires that should be carried forward. Activity sheet 18 allows pupils to use the conquistador image to record both the reasons for wanting an empire and methods of control ('big questions' 1 and 2), using colour coding. Pupils should understand that while the Romans and Spanish shared a wish for individual fame and fortune, land, riches and new resources and both used force initially, there were also differences in their motives and means of establishing control:

- Cortes was primarily an adventurer
- the conquistadors in the sixteenth century were not aiming to set up peaceful, law-abiding colonies of native people
- in the Spanish empire, wealth came from taking silver, gold and other natural resources but not from taxation
- the Romans were not concerned with spreading religious ideas but extending Christianity was important to the Spanish
- the Romans established themselves alongside the Britons, using slaves and sending many back to Rome; the Spanish became landowners in Mexico and, having wiped out the Native Americans, had to import slaves.

These points are re-visited in 'Comparing empires' on page 63.

How did the Spanish Empire affect people?
This third key question is summarised using the skittles activity, once again making links back to Year 7. Pupils are meant to consider only the impact of the Spanish Conquest on the people of Mexico and not how developing an empire affected the Spanish people in Spain, so the activity questions can easily be covered in discussion. Activity sheet 19 could be completed as a written record.
The information on pages 60–61 will probably lead pupils to knock over skittles 1, 2, 3, 4 and 5; skittles 6, 7 and 9 will probably be left standing; 8 and 10 could totter – though pupils should be encouraged to debate the issues. Here is a summary:
1. **Population:** Native Americans in Mexico wiped out; many Spaniards started to explore and move to colonies
2. **Ideas and religion:** Aztec culture replaced by Christianity

3. **Freedom:** before disease hit the population, the Aztecs were subjugated by force
4. **Education:** Aztecs were forced to convert to Christianity
5. **Work:** slavery and working for rich Spanish landowners
6. **Entertainment:** no impact
7. **Science and medicine:** no impact
8. **War:** the empire led to further wars in the Americas but war ended in Mexico because the Aztecs were wiped out
9. **Wages:** increased wealth in Spain but irrelevant to Native Americans
10. **Homes, clothes and food:** the Spanish took their fashion and building styles to Mexico; wealth led to new building in Spain.

Finally, two minutes should be enough time for pupils to refer back to their conquistador diagram or the information on page 62 to find the answers for the questions in the 'Comparing empires' section.

Plenary

Doing History: Interpretations
Teaching interpretations has been a frequently neglected part of the History curriculum. It is important that the four points, two recapped from previous learning (page 64) and the two new ideas on page 65, are understood and re-visited as pupils work through KS3, starting with the British Empire in the next lesson sequence. It would be worth making a display of the four points, perhaps asking pupils to create a poster for each one. For example:
- People tell different stories or interpretations of the past –
  Grandad telling grandson about school: "I was really well-behaved"; teacher telling grandson about his grandad at school: "He was a terrible show-off".
- People create different interpretations by including some people, topics or evidence and leaving out or down-playing others –
  Grandad telling grandson about school: "I won the drama prize"; teacher telling grandson about his grandad at school: "He was always in detention".
- Interpretations are determined by the attitudes and beliefs of the person creating the interpretation –
  White American commenting on photo of Barack Obama's inauguration: "This shows

the world that Americans are not racist";
Black American commenting on picture of
Barack Obama's inauguration: "This shows
the world that wealth and education can
overcome racial prejudice".
- Interpretations can be controversial –
Both the above comments are unfair because
they only tell a small part of the story.
Activity 1 on page 64 will be quite challenging
for some pupils and careful thought should be
given to the way the class is grouped. For
example:
- there is an opportunity for gifted and
talented pupils to take a leading role,
though they need to be guided in how to do
this. Being the group leader does **not** mean
doing all the work but gives him/her
responsibility for ensuring that all members
of the group are involved and understand
the task
- weaker groups could be asked to represent
the Aztec warrior and the conquistador, as
their attitudes are probably more
straightforward than the modern equivalents
- teacher support could be given to groups of
pupils who struggle with such concepts,
leaving other groups to work more
independently
- a group of the most able pupils would be
expected to produce a more sophisticated
analysis than those of mixed ability.
The activity needs really focused preparation
lasting no more than 20 minutes (and,
depending on the class, this could be less) to
prepare notes for the speaker/s. The minute
taken for telling the story is better used if each
member of the group makes one or two points,
ensuring all participate.
Pupils will need to refer back to the
information on pages 55–59 and to their own
report from that lesson.
Each story should look at their character's
interpretation of:

a) first impressions and reception by the Aztecs
– initial amazement on both sides; Aztec
hospitality and mutual sharing of
experiences
b) changing attitudes – increasing disgust of
Spanish at some Aztec practices compared to
Aztec pride in their culture and traditions
c) fighting and war – Spanish would probably
consider eventual victory to be certain,
despite being outnumbered, because of the
Aztecs' 'primitive' weapons; Aztecs would
note the advantage of long steel swords etc.
Both sides would consider they fought
fiercely and with courage
d) outcomes – the Spanish would focus on their
success and subsequent power and wealth,
the Aztecs on the way they were treated and
then wiped out.
Activity sheet 20 provides a word bank which
will support weaker pupils.
Note: If time permits the stories could be made
into posters or four-box comic strips to use as
display for the key points about interpretations.
However, the concentration on presentation
could easily prevent appropriately deep
thinking about the different perspectives of
each character, so it would not be a good
alternative to the oral interpretation and
discussion.
Activity 2 on page 65 provides the link with the
next lesson sequence.

Assessment for Learning – Outcomes to look for

a) Can pupils explain the concept of empire?
b) Can they recall the three key questions on
empire and suggest some answers?
c) Can they give an example of an historical
interpretation and start to explain why it is a
particular version of an event?

The British Empire and the slave trade

Summary	This enquiry starts with a brief introduction to the British Empire but the greater part of the sequence is a study of the slave trade, slavery and the struggle for their abolition. These are revealed through Thomas Clarkson's campaign and then by consideration of the part played by William Wilberforce. The important role of black men and women and a brief look at modern day slavery are included. Pupils have to make a speech and plan a documentary to explain their learning.
Time needed	This is a depth study and will require adequate time allocation to complete properly. Depending on the number and length of lessons per week possibly up to a full half-term will be needed.
Key concepts and processes	**Interpretations:** versions of the story of the slave trade **Enquiry; Evidence:** the Clarkson Challenge **Communicating about the past:** making a speech; preparing a documentary **An opportunity to explore ways in which the past has helped to shape attitudes today**
Resources	• Pupil's Book pages 66–89 • Activity sheets 21–26

Objectives

By the end of this depth study pupils should be able to:
• give reasons why the Empire was important to Britain
• give reasons why the slave trade was important to Britain
• understand and be able to exemplify how historians and others form interpretations
• suggest why the slave trade is often interpreted in different ways
• select relevant and appropriate sources for particular tasks and begin to evaluate them.

Lesson sequence

Why were the British so worried about their empire in the 1780s? (pages 66–67)
This is a straightforward Q&A activity which should take no more than 10 minutes. It

provides background information for the depth study. The questions could be revisited before moving on to look at the British Empire again on page 90.

The task should be started with a recap of pupils' knowledge about empires, the key points being:
• the Romans and Spanish gained their empires by taking land from native peoples by force
• colonies and trade then followed
• war against other empire builders meant some land changed hands
• the British gained many colonies in the same way, though a significant part of Britain's empire also grew from the establishment of trading posts in the first instance.

Note: The map shows the British Empire in about 1780 but the first attempts to build an empire dated back to the sixteenth century and the American colonies had been under British control for well over 150 years before they demanded independence.

Starter

What made Thomas Clarkson so angry? (pages 68–69)
The picture clues on these pages have been chosen to intrigue pupils and promote discussion.

The essay topic was slavery, clearly suggested by clues 1–3, clue 4 (the sugar at the tea party), clue 5 (the man's pipe tobacco) and clue 6 (Cape Coast Castle, built in West Africa for holding slaves until the ships sailed). Clue 7 is the plan of the slave ship *Brookes*, showing just how tightly packed in the slaves were as they were transported.

In addition to the images, this could be an opportunity to use some artefacts, which always stimulate interest.

- Very few pupils will have seen real sugar cane, available in some specialist shops and markets (especially West Indian ones), online and, in some places, as parrot food!
- Many museums have loan services, providing boxes of treasures that pupils can handle and they may well have sugar clippers, clay pipes, sugar tongs, etc.
- Though not relevant to this part of the enquiry, several places have gruesome replicas of leg-irons, thumbscrews and whips, etc. available to borrow or to go and see.
- The most adventurous teachers, with time to spare(!), may like to try making a cone-shaped sugar loaf – trial and error are needed, plus minimal quantities of water and about two days for it to dry out and harden. In the interests of cross-curricular co-operation, the food technology department may be willing to help!

Development

How did the slave trade work? (pages 70–71)
What did Thomas Clarkson's research tell him?
What was being carried round the 'Triangle'?
The study of the slave trade starts with the triangular trade map. Activity sheet 21 allows pupils to add notes to their own copy of the map.

a) Voyage 1 – cloth, metal, guns and alcohol
b) Voyage 2 – slaves, *c.*80,000 per annum
c) Voyage 3 – sugar and tobacco. Some pupils may know that cotton was also produced on

plantations and taken back to provide the raw material for the Lancashire cotton mills and, though this is not mentioned here, it could be added.

d)

Clue	Stage of Triangular Trade
2	2/3
3	2
4	3
5	3
6	1/2
7	2

The Clarkson Challenge (pages 72–81)
This is a demanding series of activities that builds towards the pupils making a speech for which detailed guidance is given on pages 80–81. Pupils need to be made aware of the enquiry outcome at the start and that they are gathering evidence about the slave trade, which they will use to persuade others of its evils.

Challenge 1
'Who benefited?' cards and a master for the ripple diagram, which would be better photocopied to A3 size, are available as Activity sheets 22 and 23. There is no 'right order' for this activity, though it should generate important discussion, leading to recognition that there were powerful forces ranged against the anti-slavery campaign.

Challenge 2
The arguments put forward to defend the slave trade (also shown on Activity sheet 24) could be introduced more dramatically if there are five articulate and confident pupils who could read each one aloud, as if in role. They could be put in the 'hot seat' at various intervals through the enquiry. Having heard the arguments, the rest of the class could then be challenged to find support for their peers from Sources 1–3 on page 74.

1. Source 1 is evidence for defence of the slave trade [4]
   Source 2 is evidence for defence of the slave trade [1] – slaves are happy doing undemanding work
   Source 3 is evidence for defence of the slave trade [5] – clean, well-fed, healthy slaves are happy relaxing on the plantation.
2. Clarkson could challenge the reliability of the sources by saying:
- Captain Norris's job depends on the slave trade – he is hardly likely to admit to inhuman conditions and treatment
- Plantation owners would say that, wouldn't they?

But also – slaves had to be obedient and had no choice of activity, so perhaps they aimed to make the best of a bad situation
And – a manual for plantation owners was obviously designed to encourage and reassure new slave owners
- The plantation owner wanted an attractive picture to put on his wall – it was not intended as an accurate record.
He would want to show off his 'property' to others back in Britain.

The artist would know how to please and would want to ensure payment for his work.
Challenge 3
The table from page 75 is available on Activity sheet 25 to save pupils unnecessary time copying it out, but it may need to be increased to A3 size to give adequate space for all the information. The first column has been completed but pupils need to find specific examples from Clarkson's notebooks and other witnesses as supporting evidence, as shown below.

Evidence found against the defence of the slave trade:

Argument put forward to defend the slave trade	Your counter argument	Supporting evidence	Witness
1 Africans were less skilled than Europeans – white people were superior	African kingdoms before the arrival of Europeans were just as advanced as those in Europe	The kingdom of Ghana controlled a huge empire, traded in gold and salt and had an army of 200,000 men. The kingdom of Benin showed that people were highly skilled in ivory carving, pottery and gum production. The kingdom of Mali was 2000km wide and traded in gold dust and agricultural produce. The Songhay kingdom had an organised system of government, centred on the city of Timbuktu, which had libraries and universities.	Thomas Clarkson
2 The slave trade made lots of money for Britain. Africa was undeveloped so no other trade there was possible	There were great benefits to be had from trade with Africa, without the need for capturing and selling slaves	Trade could be established in crafted ivory goods, woven and dyed cloth, pepper, beeswax and palm oil. Africa had rice, grain, fruit, fish and fine crafts. African produce included cinnamon, tobacco and cotton.	Thomas Clarkson John Wesley Seen in the painting by A E Chalon
3 Slaves were not captured cruelly	Slaves were very poorly treated when they were captured	Africans were seized without warning. They were forced to march great distances, joined by chains or neck yokes. Many died on the journey to the coast. The water they were given to drink was often stagnant.	Olaudah Equiano John Clarkson (Thomas' brother)

4 Conditions on the slave ships were good	Conditions on the ship were dreadful	Slaves were often thrown overboard from the slave ship *Zong* because they were sick or dying.	Granville Sharp
		The holds in slave ships were overcrowded, there was no room for people to move, the air was foul and the smell disgusting. Slaves were chained. They only had buckets for toilets. Beatings were used as punishment and many died during the voyage.	Olaudah Equiano
		Slaves developed sores from lying on bare planks. The deck was covered in mucus and blood and resembled a slaughterhouse.	Thomas Clarkson after speaking to a ship's surgeon
		The 'tools of the trade' were handcuffs, leg irons, thumbscrews and devices to enable force-feeding.	Olaudah Equiano
		The plan of the ship *Brookes* shows how tightly the slaves were packed in.	Thomas Clarkson
5 Enslaved Africans were treated well on the plantations	Slaves were not treated well by plantation owners	Slaves were not fed properly. Life expectancy was only 26 years. They were very likely to catch fatal diseases. Children often worked from the age of 7 or 8. Adults often worked 6 days a week and 12 hours a day. There were very harsh punishments, including death, branding, whipping, or having their ear nailed to a pot, for those who ran away or did not work hard enough.	Thomas Clarkson, after talking to James Ramsay

Challenge 4
There is a very detailed structure given on page 80 for pupils to follow when drafting their own speech, using all the evidence they have recorded and William Pitt's oratorical skills as a model. Teachers should go through this with the class.
The story of abolition – how should it be told? (pages 82–88)
This part of the lesson sequence presents pupils with another opportunity to study a controversial interpretation, one that gives the credit for ending slavery in the British colonies to William Wilberforce, who was responsible for introducing the first anti-slave trade bill to Parliament but was only one among many who brought about successful abolition.

There is a danger that pupils view the slaves and free black African men and women as weak and oppressed victims, who were first bullied by white people and then 'rescued' by them, but this is far from the truth, so it is especially important to study their part in the abolition story.
In order to challenge the traditional interpretation presented on page 82, the pupils are asked to consider many thought-provoking questions. The activity is intended as an introduction to creating their own proposal for a documentary, which will involve addressing several of the issues raised in more depth. Each of the challenges could therefore be allocated to small groups who would decide if the

challenge was justified, then in turn briefly feed back their reasons to the class.

Although the activity only requires the creation of a proposal for their documentary, realisation of a two-minute trailer, using MovieMaker or similar, could be motivating for many pupils, if there is adequate ICT resource available. The trailer would feature snapshots of the most important moments from the documentary.

Proposal for the documentary

- This would work well as a paired activity. Having some debate about the relative importance of different elements of the story is essential but larger groups may lead to some pupils 'opting out' of the discussion or finding it difficult to reach a consensus.
- Adequate time will have to be allowed to do the activity properly and pupils will need to revise their drafts several times. They may be reluctant ... but drafting and redrafting is part of the learning.
- Activity sheet 26 is an outline of the proposal table. Pupils will need several copies of this sheet – or they could use ICT to save their different versions. Each version of the proposal should be saved to show the development in their thinking.

First draft – drawn up based on the challenges from page 83 and the 'road' of seven key events on the way to abolition shown on page 84. One possible example:

1. Introduction – put slavery into context, showing that it had existed throughout history. Give background information on Africa before the European slave trade began. (7 mins.)
2. Describe the seventeenth/eighteenth century European slave trade – where from/to, etc. (6 mins.)
3. 1791 – introduce Wilberforce and the first bill to abolish the trade. (5 mins.)
4. 1804–1807 – introduce Clarkson and his evidence against the slave trade, focusing on the capture and transport of slaves, rather than conditions on the plantations. (12 mins.)
5. Describe and explain the opposition – British vested interest; huge profits, etc. (5 mins.)
6. 1807 Abolition of the Slave Trade Act. (5 mins.)
7. Life on plantations – why the 1807 Act was only part of the solution. (5 mins.)
8. 1823 Anti-Slavery Society – increasing number of members and general support. (6 mins.)
9. 1833 Abolition of slavery in the British Empire – could mention that this did not apply in the USA. (4 mins.)
10. A look at the situation today. (5 mins.)

Second draft – it should be clear, from the information on pages 85 and 86, that other important campaigners must be included in the documentary, both at the Anti-Slave Trade stage and in the 1820s. This will require quite tricky adjustments, especially in the timings. For example:

- less time could be taken to explain the mechanics of the trade (stage 2)
- Clarkson & Wilberforce could be introduced as a duo at stage 3, with other campaigners taking the leading role in stage 4 – Equiano, Sharp, Cugoano and Dolben.
- Less time could be given to stages 5 and 6 – though the importance of the Act of 1807 must not be neglected, as it was certainly a very significant first step and may be regarded as a 'turning point' (see question 2, page 84).
- This would give a little more time for anti-slavery campaigners from the 1820s – Mary Prince, Elizabeth Heyrick, religious groups (stage 8).

Third draft – it is important, as has been mentioned, not to ignore the part the slaves themselves played, so the probable final version has to include slave resistance, using the two case studies from page 87.

These would fit most easily into stage 7 and, to allow appropriate coverage, time will need to be trimmed off other sections – for example, the introduction and perhaps stage 9, the actual Act being of less importance than the efforts to achieve it.

Final version – this will not vary greatly from draft 3 but should bring the story right up to date (stage 10), using the information from page 88.

Plenary

Doing History: Interpretations
Why do we have to be careful telling the story of the slave trade?
Questions 1–3 are for discussion and build on 'Doing History: Interpretations' pages 64–65. Question 2: Point out that African and Caribbean audiences will understandably want

to emphasise examples of black heroism and campaigning but that they will also be more *interested* in the history of their own country and ancestors than in studies centred on Britain.

Question 3: Hopefully, most, if not all, pupils will have an anti-racist perspective and some may be of Afro-Caribbean origin – apart from other diverse attitudes.

What can we learn from the campaign to abolish slavery about how to run a modern-day campaign?

Instant reaction will be that modern technology has revolutionised present day methods so that there can be no similarities – millions can hear about injustice very quickly.

Pupils will need to include techniques that use 21st-century communication among their ideas. In fact, campaigns in the past and present both require:

- collection of evidence to prove the rightness of the cause, checked by interviews with witnesses and site visits
- support from influential people and those in positions of power, often obtained by personal approach and petitioning

- support from large numbers of the general public, who can be rallied at meetings, through speeches and on marches
- wearing down of opposition from those with vested interest in maintaining the status quo.

There is no denying the power of the internet, mass media and mobile phones, but sometimes people don't listen, don't want to hear or don't want to be involved … probably less has changed than might at first appear.

⮀❯ Assessment for Learning – Outcomes to look for

a) Can pupils give some reasons why the Empire and slave trade were important to Britain?

b) Can pupils explain why the slave trade and the British Empire are often interpreted differently by different people with different experiences?

c) Have pupils selected relevant and appropriate sources for the various tasks?

d) Can pupils explain why some of sources are better than others for particular tasks?

Summary	This short enquiry provides an overview of some positive and negative aspects of the British Empire. The Big Story looks at the reasons why Europeans considered empires to be important and at different opinions held by some of those affected by empire.
Time needed	1–2 hours
Key concepts and processes	**Interpretations:** the British Empire
Resources	• Pupil's Book pages 90–97 • Activity sheets 27–29

Objectives

By the end of this enquiry pupils should:
- be able to explain some positive and negative aspects of the British Empire, at home and in the colonies
- understand why people disagree about empires in general and the British Empire in particular.

Lesson sequence

Starter

After studying the slave trade, this section returns to the more general story of the British Empire.

For teachers who are comfortable with role play, a hook for this can be a simulation of a late-Victorian classroom, set up as below:

1. *The classroom desks or tables need to be arranged into rows of 'benches', split down the middle into a boys' half and a girls' half.*
2. *Additional furniture and artefacts could include a lectern, cane, dunce's hat, sampler or religious tract for display, picture of Queen Victoria, etc.*
3. *If possible the teacher should wear token Victorian costume – pupils are always impressed by a gown and mortar board, though these were really only worn by the men in grammar schools. Cloth caps and pinafores could also be worn by any willing pupils.*

4. *Of importance for this particular lesson is the map of the British Empire from 1900, easily found online and projected so that it is of similar size to those used in Victorian classrooms.*
5. *The lesson starts with the chanting of the names of colonies, when indicated on the map by the teacher.*
6. *The* pièce de résistance *for the pupils is using dip pens and ink. Modern dip pens retain ink quite well and are actually quite easy to write with, without making huge inkblots. Blotting paper can be bought in large sheets from stationers and it's quite likely that at least one member of staff has hoarded some of the small, plastic film containers, from the pre-digital camera age, which make ideal ink wells – do not put more than a minute amount of ink in each one in case of spills!*
7. *Activity sheet 27 could be copied out in 'perfect copperplate'.*

Those who prefer not to use role play, as above, could still introduce pupils to the Empire using a Victorian map, explaining the pride most people felt in being British and having such influence.

Development

Why were people so proud of the British Empire in 1900? (pages 90–95)

There is a fair amount of information in the little stories that make up the big picture of the British Empire on pages 90–95. The activity on page 90 could be divided up so that a third of the class look for a) parts of the story that get the 'thumbs up', a third look for b) parts that get the 'thumbs down' and a third find c), stories that are likely to be interpreted differently. Alternatively the class could be split into two groups, leaving c) for the whole class to debate, after they have had a chance to familiarise themselves with the stories from looking at a) or b). After a set time a representative from each group, using their

own flip chart or equivalent with the relevant logos drawn at the top, could take suggestions for their list. Activity sheet 28 can be used to record answers. These would then form the basis for discussion of questions 2 and 3 of the activity, the answers to which should be written up by pupils individually in the end.
The lists should probably look something like this:

Thumbs up	Open to interpretation	Thumbs down
Empire sports	Dominion status for Canada, Australia, New Zealand and South Africa	Lack of equality for native people's sports teams
Medical improvements in Fiji	Transportation of convicts to Australia	Violence of the Indian revolt
End of suti in India	Spread of Christianity	Removal of ruler of Benin by force
Lansdowne railway bridge in Pakistan	Indian soldiers in World War One	Taking of land from Aborigines and killing many
Schools in Pakistan	18-year-old Sultan of Zanzibar under control of British	Maoris' loss of land in New Zealand
Medical officer in Nigeria		Death of Fijians from measles
Trade, leading to job creation and increased standards of living in Britain		Looting in Mandalay
Huge range of foods available		Cheating and subsequent treatment of King Lobengula and Ndebele people in what became Rhodesia
Imports brought huge range of goods to Britain and sent money back to the colonies		Lack of respect for and harsh treatment of people in Africa

Plenary

The Big Story: Empire Part Two (pages 96–97) is summarised by looking for similarities and differences between attitudes towards empires. Activity 1 looks at three reasons Europeans had for believing empires were important.

- Reason 1: applied to all three empires
- Reason 2: would not apply to Rome
- Reason 3: the Romans may easily have shared this post-Industrial Revolution attitude!

Activity sheet 29 can be used to record answers to Activity 2 and is a brief test of pupils' understanding of the impact empires have had. Comments should be assigned as below:

- Roman general – 1, 5
- Briton under Roman rule – 2, 3 (answers might depend on which period of Roman occupation)
- Aztec – 2, 4
- conquistador – 1, 5, 6
- British politician – 1, 7
- Indian in the British Empire – 2, 3, 4, 6, but this could very much depend on individual experiences and circumstances.

Learning Log (page 97)
This records the key ideas about empires that pupils need to carry forward from the work they have done.

⬍⟩ Assessment for Learning – Outcomes to look for

a) Can pupils give some reasons why the Victorians were so proud of their empire?

b) Can pupils give reasons why the British Empire could still be regarded as having had a positive impact on the world?

c) Can pupils explain some reasons why the British Empire is often interpreted differently now?

d) Can pupils give examples of people who would have different opinions about the British Empire and explain why?

SECTION 3 OVERVIEW
MOVEMENT AND SETTLEMENT: INTO THE UNKNOWN: WERE ALL EMIGRANTS BRAVE AND ADVENTUROUS?

This section continues the thematic story of movement and settlement introduced in Year 7 and gives pupils an opportunity to consider the diversity of different people's experiences at different times.

◆⟩ Lesson sequence 8: Movement and settlement into the unknown: were all emigrants brave and adventurous? (pp. 98–111)

Why did people leave Britain? Three case studies suggest different reasons – pupils have to consider the dangers of generalisation and the links that can be made with the Big Story.

<table>
<tr><td>

Plan for lesson sequence 8
</td><td>

Movement and settlement: Into the unknown: were all emigrants brave and adventurous?
</td></tr>
<tr><td>

Summary
</td><td>

This enquiry focuses on the reasons for, and results of, emigration from Britain between 1500–1900.

Three case studies – the Pilgrim Fathers; eighteenth- century Canadian Scots and nineteenth-century Irish emigration – are used to provide answers to the questions.

'Doing History' is about diversity and generalisation.

Part 2 of Movement and Settlement is a summary of the Big Stories about emigration. The enquiry ends by making links between the stories of Movement and Settlement and those of Ordinary Life, Conflict, Empire and Power.
</td></tr>
<tr><td>

Time needed
</td><td>

3 hours
</td></tr>
<tr><td>

Key concepts and processes
</td><td>

Cause and consequence: reasons and results of emigration
Diversity: varied experiences of different groups of people
</td></tr>
<tr><td>

Resources
</td><td>

- Pupils Book pages 98–111
- Activity sheets 30–32
</td></tr>
</table>

Objectives

By the end of this enquiry pupils should be able to:
- explain reasons for and results of emigration, supporting ideas with some examples
- identify and give examples of the diversity of peoples' experiences
- understand what is meant by a generalisation
- understand that generalisations need to be tested and supported by evidence.

Lesson sequence

Starter

For the activity on page 98 pupils should:
- work out why four different groups of people from four different time periods decided to emigrate
- think of a variety of adjectives that could be used to describe the emigrants
- start their own word bank, as this would be a valuable aid throughout the enquiry and especially for the plenary

- be encouraged to think of questions, regardless of the probability of finding the answers, for example:
  a) Were all Monmouth's rebels men?
  b) Do any of Monmouth's rebels have descendants in Barbados?
  c) Who lived in Patagonia before the Welsh arrived?
  d) Did the emigrants inter-marry with the indigenous population?

Development

Investigating the lives of emigrants from Britain (pages 100–107)
The three key questions for this enquiry are introduced, each having a different diagram for recording answers (see Activity sheets 30A–C – the diagrams should ideally be increased to at least A3 size).

Information comes from the four examples on pages 98–99 and from the three case studies. Instructions on how to carry out the investigation are very clearly explained in the Activity box on page 100.

Question 1: Why did they emigrate?
- The Pilgrim Fathers belong to the beliefs section of the Venn diagram
- Canadian Scots went for economic reasons
- The Irish were forced by starvation and because of their economic circumstances.

Question 2: How were they received in their new land?
There is not much information in the first four examples about how the emigrants were received but:
- after a time the Roman army were usually accepted, but not welcomed
- Monmouth's rebels were used, rather than welcomed. They were regarded as criminals and were quite probably treated with some hostility
- the Welsh families seemed to settle peacefully and may have been helped by the native people of Patagonia
- the account says the children from children's homes had a neutral reception on the whole.

The case studies show that:
- the Pilgrim Fathers had a mixed reception, being both attacked and helped by Native Americans – they could have two entries on the diagram
- Canadian Scots struggled on their own
- many Irish were regarded with suspicion and hostility, at least initially.

Question 3: What effects did their arrival have on their new land?
All emigrants experienced massive changes to their personal lives but not all had a significant impact on their new home land.
- Individual British Roman soldiers did not settle as a group in new countries and therefore did not bring about significant change
- Monmouth's rebels provided labour for the plantations and in that way helped to develop Barbados, but it was not through their own positive and successful actions
- The Welsh families worked hard and settled successfully but were absorbed into Patagonia rather than bringing about new development
- The children in Canada increased the number of colonists and many of their descendants saw it become a developed and modern nation but the children themselves had little chance to effect change
- The Pilgrim Fathers established New England, leading the way for thousands of emigrants and the emergence of the USA

- The Scots emigrants created the new colony of Nova Scotia and made a huge contribution to the development of Canada
- The Irish were absorbed into America and helped to fill jobs in the new and growing colonies.

Doing History: Diversity and generalisation (pages 108–109)
Diversity and generalisation have been linked together because pupils have to learn that, because of the diversity of peoples' experiences, people should be treated as individuals but that, in practice, it would be impossible to study history without grouping people together and making general statements about them. Pupils need to be taught to recognise such generalisations and to make sure they are as accurate as possible by testing them, strengthening them and making sure they choose their words carefully. This section goes through these points, using the diagrams completed during their investigation into emigration for support.

Step 1: Pupils should conclude that the generalisation in the statement given is partly true. Economic reasons were a very important consideration for many emigrants but not the only one.

Steps 2 and 3: Pupils must use their diagrams for evidence and check the case studies for any detail needed.

Step 4: It would be useful to have the qualifying words on A4 or A5 cards, displayed in the classroom and certainly pupils should have their own list (Activity sheet 31) for easy reference. They could also be used as flash cards in brief starters or plenaries.
Ask, for example, who (which team/which pair) can:
- 'add the most qualifying words to this sentence, without making it nonsense?'
- 'make this sentence more accurate?'
- 'modify this sentence most quickly?'
- 'make up sentences that include … the teacher shuffles the word cards and selects one or two at random]?'

Sentences could be topic related or more general:
Emigrants had reasons for going to America.
Jack the Ripper was a doctor who killed prostitutes.
Medieval kings were boys.
King Henry loved his wives.
Young people mug old ladies for fun.

On your own (page 108)
The statement that emigrants were welcomed and helped by the people already there (question 2, page 101) is probably an easier choice for this final task on page 108 because the statement following question 3 does not so clearly link with the diagram.

Learning Log
Pupils may find it quite hard to explain these ideas for their Learning Log as they need to record the general points which underpin the work they have done using specific examples. Using their own words they should try to explain:
- what is meant by a generalisation
- why they are made
- why and how they can be strengthened.

Plenary

The Big Story: Movement and Settlement Part Two (pages 110–111)
Pupils should be able to answer the questions in the activity box on page 110 without difficulty, especially if they did build up a word bank as they worked through this enquiry. Reading through the key questions and summaries with the class will allow the teacher to ask for specific examples as answers for each one. Pupils can use knowledge from their work on empires in addition to the case studies used for the enquiry. Activity 2: Activity sheet 32 is available as a template for this diagram.

Using the four examples of emigration given on page 111 as models, pupils could make three more 'cards', one for each case study, along the lines of:

E) *In the early seventeenth century, Puritans wanted to worship in their own way and when this was not allowed some decided to set up their own community in America. They are known as the Pilgrim Fathers.*

F) *In the eighteenth century Britain needed colonists to settle in Canada. Many poor Scots were attracted by the scheme organised by the British government, which enabled them to start a new, and hopefully better, life in Canada, very cheaply.*

G) *More than a million starving Irish men, women and children went to America in the mid-nineteenth century after potato blight caused famine in Ireland.*

All seven examples can then be added to the diagram:

Ordinary life – E, F, G	Empires – D, F
Conflicts – A, B	Power: monarchy and democracy – A, C

Notes for the connecting lines could be:
Ordinary people emigrated
- *because of their beliefs*
- *to improve their lives.*

Empires offered
- *new land*
- *new opportunities*
- *adventure.*

Conflicts
- *sometimes made life very difficult for people to stay in Britain.*

Power: monarchy and democracy
- *sometimes people were forced to emigrate because they did not fit in with the governments of the time.*

Learning Log
It may be helpful to point out that the reasons for people emigrating from Britain were often very similar to the reasons other people had for a) leaving their own countries, or b) being attracted to Britain.

⟩⟩ Assessment for Learning – Outcomes to look for

a) Can pupils explain reasons for and results of emigration, supporting ideas with some examples?

b) Can pupils identify and give examples of how people's experiences differ?

c) Can pupils explain what is meant by 'generalisation'?

d) Can pupils give an example of a generalisation and show how it could be tested and supported with evidence?

Linked web-based activities

Why did they go to America?
http://www.thinkinghistory.co.uk/ActivityBase/WhyDidTheyGoToAmerica.html

SECTION 4 OVERVIEW
CONFLICT: WHICH WARS SHOULD WE KNOW ABOUT?

This section provides an overview of wars between 1500 and 1900, looking at cause and consequence through the study of two examples in depth. Then Top Trumps cards give pupils a chance to decide which wars they think were most significant and worthy of study.

♦> Lesson sequence 9: Invasion attempts (pp. 112–129)

Pupils hypothesise about the reasons for the failure of Spanish and French attempts at invasion in the sixteenth and early nineteenth centuries and test their theories against the evidence they collect.

♦> Lesson sequence 10: Which wars? A quick history of war and peace (pp. 130–139)

An overview of 24 wars in which Britain has been involved, from the 1066 Norman Conquest to the 21st-century Iraq War.

Invasion attempts

Summary	This enquiry, including Doing History, is about causation and the links that can be made between reasons for historical events. There are two case studies, on Philip II's attempted invasion of Britain in 1688 and Napoleon's in 1805, that include interesting details about guns and military tactics, which might especially appeal to boys, and provide good opportunities for active learning (non violent!). The main aim is to develop pupils' skills in the creation and testing of hypotheses and a clear structure is given for this, leading to the final write-up.
Time needed	About 3 hours
Key concepts and processes	**Causation:** reasons for failure of invasion attempts **Historical enquiry:** making and testing hypotheses
Resources	• Pupil's Book pages 112–129 • Activity sheets 33–35

Objectives

By the end of this enquiry pupils should be able to:
• identify and assess the relative importance of reasons why the two invasion attempts failed
• explain some links between the reasons for these failures
• start devising their own hypotheses about these events
• refine their hypotheses after testing them against the evidence.

Lesson sequence

Starter (page 112)

The quiz is included for recap purposes only and should be done quickly. The questions could be used in various game formats – think of popular TV shows. It is also relatively easy to find online inter-active quiz templates that teachers can modify by adding their own questions. Another simple idea is the 'Football (or basketball, hockey, etc.) Pitch'.

1. Draw a football pitch on the whiteboard with a centre line, a goal at each end and two or three circles randomly scattered between the centre and the goal, which represent possible passes of the ball as the team tries to score.
2. Divide the class into two teams.
3. Toss a coin to decide who starts.
4. The teacher reads out the questions and the team that 'kicks off' has the chance to answer until they make a mistake – a different member of the team must 'pass the ball' (answer the question) each time.
5. For each correct answer they can move the ball one space towards the goal.
6. If they 'score' the ball returns to the centre and the other team restarts the game.
7. If a team gets an answer wrong, the ball goes to the opposition, but they must start from whichever circle play had reached, moving back towards their goal with every correct answer, until they score or make an error.
8. Play continues until the questions run out.

Answers to quiz:
1 b; **2** b; **3** a (in the summer of 1066 Harold was ready and waiting for William – by the end of summer he had allowed his men to return to their villages for harvest and on 20 September he marched north to fight off Hardrada, having reassembled a fairly strong army); **4** b; **5** a; **6** b; **7** a; **8** b; **9** b (available evidence is mixed – general consensus is that the two sides had different strengths/weaknesses but were fairly evenly matched, though some historians say Harold's army was smaller, as he had lost many men at Stamford Bridge and on his march south); **10** a; **11** a; **12** a *or* b (his death is controversial – the arrow story is the popular version but most accounts agree he was hacked to pieces by sword, possibly after being injured by the arrow).

Development

Doing History: Causes (page 113)
Doing History provides criteria for progression, building on key points from Year 7. A table illustrating this, summarising all the Doing History pages in this Year 8 book, is available on page 99.

Why did William's invasion succeed?
- Pupils may enjoy working on the cards in pairs.
- Discuss ideas about what could be written on each card.
- Keep to time limits both for choosing the information for each card (15–20 minutes in total) and for deciding how to arrange them (3–5 minutes).
- Activity sheet 33 suggests possible endings for cards, if required.

There is no correct answer for the arrangement of the cards – the importance of the activity lies in justifying choices and making links. Time should be given for such feedback.
Possible links could be:
Planning ←→ Leadership – a good leader will plan and prepare carefully
Planning ←→ Fighting forces/Weapons
Leadership ←→ Fighting forces – inspiring men; ensuring adequate resources
Leadership ←→ Weapons – adequate resources
Fighting forces ←→ Weapons – one is no good without the other
Luck ←→ any of the other factors – these can all be changed by good/bad luck

Why did the Spanish Armada fail?
(pages 114–121)
There are two case studies in this enquiry – the Spanish Armada and the Battle of Trafalgar. Both require pupils to use the same techniques and, if there are time constraints, it may be worth considering splitting the class, with half studying the Armada and half Trafalgar. Further help with this option is given below.
As an alternative to using a straight textbook explanation of the background to the Armada, the teacher could take on the role of Elizabeth I: 'What have I ever done to upset Philip?' Pupils then respond using Source 1 and the annotations.
At the end of this enquiry pupils have to write a detailed explanation of why Philip failed to invade and depose Elizabeth, based on the evidence they collect from pages 114–119. They need to recognise that success or failure depended largely on the same factors that enabled William the Conqueror to win. Having read the outline of Philip's plan pupils have to formulate a hypothesis about why it went wrong. There is no right answer – pupils should be guided to make any reasoned decision.
Steps 1 and 2 (page 115): Each pupil or pair, should be given five cards, one for each heading, ideally about A6 size (four to an A4 page) to allow space for plenty of evidence. After giving some time for collecting evidence from pages 116–117, it would be worth pausing for a brief plenary – select pupils randomly to read out one point they have recorded to see if others can identify which card it belongs to.
From the information on these two pages, pupils should find most of the following, but it does not need to be recorded in this way:
- **Planning**
  Good (for Spanish):
  1. warships moved close to target
  2. arrangements made for experienced army to be used
  3. short Channel crossing
  4. knowledge of geography of SE England.
  Bad (for Spanish):
  5. weather and English navy may interfere with 1 and 3 above
  6. will be difficult to communicate with Duke of Parma
  7. may be too confident about English defeat.

- **Fighting forces**
  Good (for Spanish):
  1. 151 ships, inc. 68 warships v. 177 smaller English ships, inc. 34 warships at sea; 34,000 soldiers to provide support for 7000 sailors v. 16,000 sailors
  2. God and 180 priests and monks on Spanish side
  3. ammunition and food for four weeks, which was longer than Spanish expected would be necessary; English may need to return to land to get more food, ammunition, etc.
  4. English land forces were badly armed and poorly trained.
  Bad (for Spanish):
  5. Philip's advisers said 500 ships were needed but too expensive
  6. English didn't believe a Roman Catholic god would help
  7. They were a long way from more supplies, if it turned out to be very long campaign
  8. English seamen were skilled and experienced.

- **Weapons**
  Good (for Spanish):
  1. cannons of different shapes and sizes
  2. soldiers armed to fight on board enemy ships.
  Bad (for Spanish):
  3. cannons took up to one hour to reload, not very suitable for use at sea v. English cannons mounted on gun carriage, reloaded in ten minutes
  4. soldiers had to board English ships but English ships used long-range guns.

- **Leadership**
  Good (for Spanish):
  1. Spanish captains were experienced sailors
  2. the English commander, Lord Howard of Effingham, was inexperienced at sea
  3. the English leaders did not know what the Spanish were planning to do.
  Bad (for Spanish):
  4. Philip could not communicate with the Armada
  5. communication between ships was difficult
  6. the Duke of Medina-Sidonia had never been to sea before
  7. Sir Francis Drake and Sir John Hawkins were brilliant seamen.

- **Luck**
  The Spanish needed good luck and good weather for the plan to succeed.

(The 'Luck' card will be completed using pages 118–119, as pupils find out what happened next.)

Once the pupils have this background evidence, they reach a 'Decision Point', providing an excellent opportunity for some active learning. See Spanish Armada, **www.thinkinghistory.co.uk**. Alternatively, you could make a model based on a map or bird's eye drawing of England, France, Spain and the Channel, with paper boats (folded similarly to newspaper hats) with straw masts and matchstick cannons. For something quicker and quieter than either of the above (but less fun!), use an interactive whiteboard – a map and a few downloaded pictures could be effective.

Using one of these methods, or just the textbook, work through to page 119, remembering to add more evidence to the cards at regular intervals:

- Planning went well in initial stages – English unable to stop Armada
- Bad luck that Parma was held up by Dutch
- Good planning and leadership by English sending in fire ships
- Spanish leaders failed to prevent panic
- Weapons on both sides not very effective
- Spanish unlucky to face strong winds, before being able to regroup
- Medina-Sidonia gave up (didn't have much choice)
- Storms and unavoidable very long homeward journey finished off Armada.

Steps 3 and 4 (page 120): Explain how pupils should test and modify their hypothesis in the light of the evidence they have collected.

Step 5 (page 121) looks at how to write good explanations, providing clear guidelines for pupils to answer the question 'Why did the Spanish Armada fail?'

Activity sheet 34 provides a writing frame.

Was Nelson the main reason why Napoleon's invasion failed? (pages 122–127)

As with the Spanish Armada, at the end of this enquiry pupils have to write a detailed explanation of why Napoleon failed to invade England, based on evidence collected from pages 122–127.

Having read the outline of Napoleon's plan from page 123 pupils formulate a hypothesis about why it went wrong: which factors – planning; leadership; fighting forces; weapons or luck – were the most and least important reasons for his failure? If pupils are studying Trafalgar as an alternative to the Armada the teacher will need to ensure they understand how to use factor cards to record their hypothesis by going through Steps 1 and 2 from page 115. As before, there is no right answer and pupils should be guided to make any reasoned decision, but the question this time implies 'leadership' was the key – they may need to be told to ignore this when formulating their own ideas.

Guidance for teachers is the same as that given for steps 1 and 2 above, using pages 123–25 to find most of the following:

- **Planning**
  Good (for Napoleon):
  1. 2000 barges arranged to carry adequate resources to England
  2. recognised need for control of the Channel
  3. knew Britain valued its colonies and successfully lured English ships away from Channel
  4. would use speed to secure victory.
  Bad (for Napoleon):
  5. British warships always on patrol in Channel
  6. reliant on quick and easy journeys across the Atlantic but many ships damaged
  7. may be too confident about English defeat.

- **Fighting forces**
  Good (for Napoleon):
  1. large number of ships – French + Spanish navies; 33 warships, some bigger than British v. 29 British warships
  2. 200,000 men.
  Bad (for Napoleon):
  3. Nelson's flagship, the *Victory*, was well-built and well armed
  4. English ships had successfully blockaded French and Spanish before
  5. Nelson's seamen were skilled and experienced
  6. many French officers were inexperienced
  7. Spanish officers and sailors did not really want to fight for Napoleon.

- **Weapons**
  Good (for Napoleon):
  1. had similar guns to British
  2. marksmen placed in rigging – proved lethal for Nelson.
  Bad (for Napoleon):
  3. British used guns to fire at hulls of enemy ships, making holes, killing men and destroying firepower – French and Spanish aimed guns at mast, rigging, etc., to stop their enemies sailing
  4. British gunners more experienced and faster at firing and reloading
  5. marksmen vulnerable and ships had to be close to enemy to be effective.

- **Leadership**
  Good (for Napoleon):
  1. Napoleon had to be obeyed.
  Bad (for Napoleon):
  2. Nelson had a reputation as a good leader and rallied fleet with famous signal
  3. British sailors were given enough to eat and drink and were kept in order without cruelty
  4. British tactics – 'crossing the T' – proved effective
  5. French captains did not feel confident.

- **Luck**
  1. not much luck involved, unless a marksman having chance to shoot Nelson was 'lucky'.

As with the Armada, a visual, interactive representation of the Battle of Trafalgar will help pupil understanding and recall of events – an adaptation of the **www.thinkinghistory.co.uk** activity, a model or use of an interactive white board – but the diagrams on page 126 are perfectly clear if these are not attractive options. The 'Think' boxes (pages 123, 124, 126, 127) provide good opportunities for mini-plenaries as pupils work through the information, and the two about Nelson are especially relevant for the final write-up.

For Steps 3, 4 and 5 refer back to pages 120–121, as above. Activity sheet 35 is a writing frame for this question.

Plenary

Now for something completely different! (pages 128–129)
The final two stories of battle in this enquiry provide a contrast to the defeat of the Armada and the British victory at Trafalgar. The discussion questions on page 129 are important and all pupils should be encouraged to think about their own responses, perhaps by considering each one in pairs, then groups of four, before feeding back to the whole class. However, pupils only have limited contextual knowledge and discussion should not be too prolonged.

Pupils could summarise by noting one reason for including the Dutch Raid and the Opium War in the curriculum and one reason for ignoring them.

Points they could think about:

- the short and long term effects of different conflicts
- the impact on the British people and/or the world at the time
- the importance of protection and promotion of British trade
- the distance from Britain – including the difference between invasion attempts and battles that held less direct threat
- the relevance of studying individual battles that were only part of much bigger wars
- the need to celebrate British success
- the need to understand that Britain suffered defeat as well as enjoying victory.

Assessment for Learning – Outcomes to look for

a) Can pupils identify five factors that could lead to success or failure in wars?
b) Can pupils explain some links between the factors leading to Philip II's failure to depose Elizabeth I with his Armada?
c) Can pupils explain some links between the factors leading to Napoleon's failure to defeat Nelson?
d) Can pupils explain why some reasons for the failure of the two invasion attempts were more important than others?
e) Do pupils understand how to devise their own hypothesis about past events?
f) Are they able to refine their hypotheses after testing them against the evidence?

Linked web-based activities

Spanish Armada
http://www.thinkinghistory.co.uk/ActivityBase/ Armada.html

<table>
<tr>
<td>

Plan for lesson sequence 10

</td>
<td>

Which wars? A quick history of war and peace

</td>
</tr>
<tr>
<td>***Summary***</td>
<td>This short lesson sequence gives an overview of 24 wars in which Britain has been involved, from the Norman Conquest in 1066 to the 21st-century Iraq War. There is then a development of the concept of significance from Year 7 in 'Doing History' and finally a consideration of how warfare and attitudes towards it have changed since the Middle Ages.</td>
</tr>
<tr>
<td>***Time needed***</td>
<td>2–3 hours</td>
</tr>
<tr>
<td>***Key concepts and processes***</td>
<td>**Significance:** what wars should be studied and what criteria applied to make that decision?
Change and continuity: what has changed about warfare and attitudes towards it?</td>
</tr>
<tr>
<td>***Resources***</td>
<td>• Pupil's Book pages 130–139
• Activity sheets 36 and 37</td>
</tr>
</table>

Objectives

By the end of this enquiry pupils should:
• recognise that some events are considered to be more significant than others
• be able to identify and give examples of criteria used to decide if events are significant
• understand that people may disagree about whether events are significant
• begin to suggest why people disagree about whether events are significant
• understand that some aspects of warfare since 1066 have changed but a few have not
• be able to suggest ways in which attitudes to war have changed over time.

Lesson sequence

The long, the short and the bloody! War and peace 1066–2000 (pages 130–133)

Starter

Activity 1 on page 130 is a quiz to allow pupils to familiarise themselves with the Top Trumps cards. Answers:
1. a) Napoleonic; b) Bonnie Prince Charlie's Rebellion; c) Napoleonic; d) Zulu; e) Crimean;
f) Marlborough's; g) Henry VIII's wars with Scotland
2. a) Seven Years; b) Marlborough's;
c) Napoleonic; d) Elizabeth I's wars with Spain
3. a) Nineteenth; b) Seven Years War; c) War of American Independence; d) Anglo-Dutch Wars;
e) Boer War.
NB The Top Trumps cards can be printed from the CD.

Development

Activity 2 (page 130):
• Unless the class is very small, pupils could work in pairs for this activity.
• The living graph, with the axes copied from page 130, must be made as large as possible – ideally it should be drawn in chalk on the floor, with the names of the wars written on tabards worn by pupils who stand in the correct place on the graph. Tabards can made from sugar paper if necessary, though having a class set of fabric tabards with a small piece of stick-on Velcro on the front to allow for different activities is very handy.
• Alternatively, cards with the names of the wars could be used on a large table-top graph or the graph could be projected onto a whiteboard.

- The whole class must be involved. If half the class are spectators, they could direct where the wars are placed.
- Task 6 answers:
  Four highest scores: Napoleonic (27); War of American Independence (23); Marlborough's (22); Seven Years War (22)
  Four lowest scores: Henry VIII's wars with Scotland (5); Bonnie Prince Charlie's Rebellion (6); War of Jenkins' Ear (6); Elizabethan wars in Ireland (7).
- Task 7 answers:
  Other wars: Elizabeth I's wars with Spain (15); Anglo-Dutch Wars (18); Opium Wars (10); Crimean War (11); Sikh Wars (11); Afghan Wars (13); Zulu War (11); Boer War (10).
- Task 9: This is an important discussion about significance!

Activity 3 (page 130):
- This is intended to be a whole-class activity, using a very large world map, possibly drawn on the floor, so all pupils can see and participate. Otherwise an interactive white board could be used or pupils could work in groups/pairs with an A3 (or similar) map.
- The best way to mark the wars is with brightly-coloured spots (or possibly 'bombs' or explosions!). This allows several to be placed in Europe, for example.
- Exact geographical position is not essential and accuracy will, in any case, depend on the size of the map. For 'all over Europe' (e.g. the Crusades), a fairly central European spot will be fine.
- Some wars will need spots in several different parts of the world.

Pupils should notice that:
- early wars were all close to home
- until the mid-eighteenth century Britain was involved in wars in Europe
- nineteenth and twentieth century wars have been more distant, including in America, Africa and Asia
- there is a link with imperial expansion.

Which British wars should you know about?/ Doing History: Significance (pages 134–135)
Significance is an important concept in the KS3 history curriculum. Here pupils build on the Year 7 definition of significance to consider what criteria wars can be measured against. Those who are also able to recognise and understand that selection of criteria can depend on attitudes and values are working at

quite a high level but able pupils should be challenged to think about this through good Q&A for question 5.

The questions in the activity are best tackled in groups, which will stimulate some debate and thought about the choices to be made.

1. Significance criteria shown round the picture of the Battle of Waterloo:
   a) 1 – scale, length of war and number of people involved
   b) 6 – proud to be British
   c) 3 – effect on other peoples and countries
   d) 2 – effect on Britain and British people
   e) 7 – a British hero
   f) 5 – proud of our soldiers' bravery.

2. As long as the group has discussed the criteria and can justify their choices, any four are possible. Despite possibly being reluctant to take the time, pupils will find it useful to have the criteria written out, rather than just having the numbers at the top of each column. Activity sheet 36 is a photocopiable version of the grid.

3. The weightings can be between 1–5 and should be added to the score given for each war, for each criterion. For example, if the group thinks that the scale of a war is far more significant than its impact on Britain and a little more important than the effect on the world, they could be weighted 5:1:3; applied to Henry VIII's wars, this would give significance scores of (2+5=)7: (1+1=)2: (2+3=)5.
   If this extra consideration causes confusion it should be omitted.

4. Complete the grid. If pupils have chosen any of the first three criteria, the points allocated for each war can be lifted from the Top Trumps cards, otherwise pupils must use their own judgement to give a mark out of 10.
   The decision about which two wars to study should then be straightforward, based on the scores allocated in the grid showing which are, in the group's opinion, the most significant.

5. There may well be different choices of criteria between groups and almost certainly different weightings and allocation of points. These can be discussed in class feedback. Reasons for the differences will be more difficult for pupils to specify but most will understand that boys may rate courage, for example, differently from girls, or those with

relatives in the forces may have different attitudes to those whose parents are pacifists.

Learning Log (page 135)

The Learning Log should be the pupil's own work but the ideas that are recorded also need to be relevant for future learning so teachers may need to give some guidance.

The main points here should be based on the three statements about significance but copying is not a good record of learning and understanding. To support the statements pupils could think about which criteria they remember and understand best – if possible generalising from the examples given to measure the significance of wars. For example: Events are significant because of their

- scale – length of time, geographical spread, numbers involved
- impact on Britain
- impact in the rest of the world
- influence on national pride about events and people
- interesting and dramatic qualities
- effect on behaviour today.

However some pupils may find it easier to record specific examples: 'The Napoleonic Wars were significant because ...'

The Big Story: Conflict and Co-operation Part Two (pages 136–137)

Learning Log

This is each pupil's own summary of the story of conflict from 1066 to 1900. Ideas they might record are:

1 Warfare

   a) changes – weapons, uniform, location, motivation

   b) continuity – location, motivation.

2 Why were wars won?

   a) changes – belief in God's support, English alliance with part of France against the rest of France, importance of naval power, industrial development and wealth

   b) continuity – weather, leadership, belief in the cause.

3 Which wars should we remember?

   a) The four characters disagree because:

   - they have chosen different criteria to decide what was significant: skill of the archers; Britain saved from threat of invasion and defeat of France; leadership of Winston Churchill and numbers of people involved; great victory

- they come from different time periods
- people from different countries will have different ideas about which wars are significant

   b) amount of threat or fear people might have felt – for example living in London or by the coast; having a relative involved; attitudes towards patriotism or the enemy.

Plenary

Conflict and co-operation: how were ideas and beliefs changing? (pages 138–139)

The table overleaf shows which pieces of evidence link to each of the attitudes shown on the timeline on page 138.

This activity could be made into a giant timeline, using the Evidence Cards from Activity sheet 37. These could be colour-coded to match the time periods. There would have to be two copies made of cards A, D, and J.

⬍⟩ Assessment for Learning – Outcomes to look for

a) Can pupils give examples of wars from the period 1500–1900 that they decided were significant?

b) Can pupils identify and give examples of criteria used to decide which wars were significant?

c) Do pupils recognise that not everyone agrees about which wars are significant or about the criteria used to decide?

d) Can pupils make some suggestions about why people disagree about which wars were significant?

e) Can pupils give examples of some of the aspects of warfare that have changed since 1066 and some aspects of warfare that have not?

f) Can pupils suggest ways in which attitudes to war have changed over time?

Linked web-based activities

A physical map showing changing geography of wars Britain was involved
http://www.thinkinghistory.co.uk/ActivityBase/ BigStoryConflicts.html

This table shows which items of evidence from page 139 should go in whch section of the timeline from page 138.

1500	1600	1700	1800	1900

It is important to stop one country taking control of the whole of Europe. If necessary we will make alliances to stop any country dominating Europe. **C, G, I**

We have a right to build up an overseas empire and trade all over the world. There is only so much wealth in the world to share so we will fight other countries to defend and increase our share of empire and trade. **B, J**

Having a strong navy is vital for defending Britain against invasion and for defending our Empire and trade throughout the world. **A, D, F**

England needs to go to war to take control of the rest of Britain. **L**

The king needs to go to war to show his people how powerful he is. **E**

Britain has become the richest nation in the world because of its empire and trade, so it needs to fight wars to protect them. **D, J**

We do not want another country to tell us what our religion should be. **A**

We cannot afford to let other countries build up industrial strength to match our own. This will threaten the British Empire and make us weaker in wars. **H, K**

SECTION 5 OVERVIEW
POWER: MONARCHY: WHEN AND WHY DID KINGS LOSE CONTROL?

This section provides an overview of the fluctuating fortunes of the English monarchy between 1500 and 1900, following on from the medieval rollercoaster of Year 7 and focusing on Change and Continuity. Enquiry skills are developed further through study of Charles I.

Lesson sequence 11: Would you have signed Charles I's death warrant? (pp. 140–149)

An enquiry developing the ability to select evidence to support judgements about what has proved to be the all-time low in the story of the monarchy – Charles I's execution.

Lesson sequence 12: The Royal Rollercoaster (pp. 150–171)

Pupils create their own image of the story of monarchy as a Royal Rollercoaster, with a focus on Change and Continuity.

Lesson sequence 13: Hero or villain? Why do reputations change over time? (pp. 172–177)

This starts with a look at Oliver Cromwell's controversial reputation and ends with a summary of the Big Story of monarchy.

Would you have signed Charles I's death warrant?

Summary	This enquiry looks at the four main charges brought against Charles I and asks pupils to weigh up the evidence and make their own judgement about the outcome. It provides pupils with a summary of the causes and events of the English Civil Wars, encouraging the selection and recording of information, which will enable pupils to justify their answers to the enquiry question.
Time needed	About 3–4 hours
Key concepts and processes	**Historical enquiry:** acquiring knowledge and selecting evidence to reach and justify conclusions
Resources	• Pupil's Book pages 140–149 • Activity sheets 38A–C, 39A and B

◗ Objectives

By the end of this enquiry pupils should be able to:
• investigate, individually or as part of a team, the question of whether Charles I deserved to be executed
• select relevant information for the enquiry
• reach and justify their own conclusions, using evidence to support their opinions.

◗ Lesson sequence

Starter (pages 140–141)

The English Civil Wars are both loved and hated by teachers. For some, the mid-seventeenth century is one of the most exciting, dramatic and significant periods of British history. For others, it is a tedious grind through 'causes', with which many pupils have difficulty empathising, briefly improved by the spectacle of a royal execution and perhaps culminating in an opportunity to 'do' an interpretation! This enquiry allows the main events to be taught quickly, while providing enough information for pupils to make a reasoned judgement about Charles I. Those who would like to study the period in more depth (and, for

example, cannot bear to miss the opportunity to show Buckingham's long, white, silky legs and pink pom-pom shoes – National Portrait Gallery) can very easily side-track temporarily before returning to the investigation as explained on page 141.

As a hook to introduce the period and the set-up of the court, it is worth showing the short trial scene from the 1970 film 'Cromwell' because, despite the horrendous historical inaccuracies of much of the film, that particular extract seems to have been well researched and uses some of the original dialogue. Many pupils also really enjoy acting out the scene and the play script produced by John Murray (Activity sheet 39B) still has much to recommend it. Pupils should be encouraged to study Source 2 carefully and to identify the key features to give them a visual context for their work.

Development (pages 142–149)

The instructions for the Activity on page 141 are clearly explained and Activity sheets 38A–C are templates for the evidence charts.
For group work, it would be best to record the evidence and defence for the activities on flip chart size paper, which could include some relevant illustrations (a ship; stained glass window; bag of gold, etc.).

At intervals, groups or individuals looking at the same charge could compare their charts and share ideas. The best or most comprehensive chart could be displayed for reference to allow all pupils to consider the whole case against Charles.

Some pupils may need to note the following, possibly in a glossary, and may need a little more

explanation of their relevance and importance:
- the phrase 'The Divine Right of Kings'
- the role of Parliament
- taxes (as opposed to taxis – not as uncommon as it should be!)
- nobles and bishops
- House of Commons and MPs.

See also Activity sheet 39A.

Charge 1: 'That he did ignore the will of Parliament and ruled according to his own will'	
Evidence against Charles	**Charles' defence**
Charles lost the trust and support of MPs	He preferred to take advice from his friends, e.g. the Duke of Buckingham
Ruled without Parliament 1629–1640	He was King by Divine Right and did not believe he had to consult anyone about the decisions he made
	Other kings had ruled without Parliament
Money – collecting taxes without permission	MPs humiliated Charles when they refused to grant customs duties for more than a year at time
Against Magna Carta	It was not actually against the law
Ship tax	Had to find ways to raise money to rule the country
Religion – to most English people, especially many Puritan MPs, Roman Catholics were enemies, who might want to make England into a Catholic country again	Charles was Protestant and did not intend to make England Catholic
Charles married a Roman Catholic princess, bringing priests and Catholic services to the Royal Court	Henrietta Maria should be allowed to worship as she chose in private
Archbishop Laud made Archbishop of Canterbury	Archbishop Laud was Protestant
Laud liked Catholic-style churches and ceremony	Even so, Laud was Protestant but liked to honour God through decoration and ritual
Charles tried to force the Scots to adopt his ideas about religion	He was King of Scotland too
The Scots invaded England	Parliament must help to defend its own country

Charge 2: '...that he did wickedly make war on his own subjects'	
Evidence against Charles	**Charles' defence**
MPs tried to discuss the issues in the Short Parliament but Charles dismissed them	He was King and must be allowed to rule his own country
	MPs were only interested in arguing about religion
Charles only called the Long Parliament because he had to	
1641 The Army Plot	MPs undermined the King's authority when they passed the Triennial Act
	He was forced to agree to the execution of his friend and most important minister, the Earl of Strafford
Charles went into the House of Commons with soldiers to arrest five leading MPs	Parliament had abolished the taxes and royal courts and were aiming to remove the rest of the King's traditional powers, and even to control the education of his children, through the Grand Remonstrance of 1641
Charles started to collect supporters and weapons	He was left with no options
Henrietta Maria went to France to raise money	Parliament issued the Militia Ordinance, raising a Parliamentary army
War began!	

Charge 3: .... that he was responsible for all the murders, rapings, burnings, damage and desolation caused by the wars	
The Royalist army were excessively violent	The Parliamentary army were excessively violent

Charge 4: ... that he restarted the war after being defeated	
Charles refused the peace agreement offered in 1646	Had to keep as much Royal power as possible
Escaped and allied with the Scots against the English, starting Second Civil War	Extremists from the Parliamentary army had taken control

Plenary

Pupils now have to return to Stage 2 on page 149. They should:

- identify their two most compelling bits of evidence
- consider questions a) and b) if they choose 'guilty'
- consider the two questions posed if they choose 'not guilty' (note: Charles has escaped before and tried to raise an army; he has refused to accept the authority of the court – the current parliament)
- not 'sit on the fence' – that is too easy!

The final vote could be taken very quickly but would be more dramatic if it was acted out with pupils taking the roles of President John Bradshaw and King Charles, using the 'script' from Activity sheet 39B. The rest of the class, as MPs, could stand in turn and cast their votes, giving their two reasons, with a clerk to the court making a tally and announcing the verdict – which John Bradshaw would have to ignore if the class opted for 'not guilty' ('*Nevertheless, the said Charles Stuart ...*'). A final dramatic gesture would be signing the death warrant with a quill. Copies of the actual document are available from HMSO and online at **www.nationalarchives.gov.uk**.

Assessment for Learning – Outcomes to look for

a) Have pupils clearly recorded evidence taken from the information available, showing a balance between the evidence against Charles and his defence?

b) Can pupils give examples and explain relevant information from the enquiry?

c) Can pupils make their own decision about Charles' guilt or otherwise?

d) Can pupils explain the reasons for their decision and give examples of the evidence they have used to form their opinions?

Linked web-based activities

Will you have finished school before Charles I is executed?
http://www.thinkinghistory.co.uk/ActivityBase/DurationTimelines.html#charles
A living graph on when decisions were taken to execute Charles I
http://www.thinkinghistory.co.uk/ActivityBase/ExecuteCharles.html

Plan for lesson sequence 12	The Royal Rollercoaster
Summary	This enquiry examines when, how and why the role of the monarchy in Britain changed so radically since the Middle Ages. Using summaries of several of the monarchs and their relationships with Parliament from the period 1500–1900, pupils have to create their own rollercoaster image. The sequence ends by asking why attitudes changed.
Time needed	2–3 hours
Key concepts and processes	**Change over time:** when, how and why the role of the monarchy changed
Resources	• Pupil's Book pages 150–171

Objectives

By the end of this enquiry pupils should be able to:
- explain changes in the role of the monarchy since 1500
- give some examples of changes and say when they took place (context or date)
- suggest reasons for the changes.

Lesson sequence

Starter (pages 150–151)

The activity offers a recap of the story of monarchy as a medieval rollercoaster. Numbered features:

1. The money showered on the king represents taxation, usually used to fund wars. Parliament Bend happens as King John faces problems with the barons, forcing him to agree to Magna Carta. They did not like the excessively heavy demands for taxation. He was followed by his son, Henry III, whose barons also rebelled, led by Simon de Montfort, who was regarded as the founder of Parliament.

2. These dips represent civil wars, when first Edward II and then Richard II lost the respect and trust of their barons and other powerful men and ended up being murdered! The tremendous twirl is the War of the Roses.

3. This refers back to the Year 7 book which looked at the role of a medieval king. In addition to being a good soldier and winning victories for England, the king was expected to keep law and order; produce at least one son and heir; get on with the barons; and get on with the Church – so anything to symbolise these could be carried by a king in the Middle Ages.

4. In medieval times there was always a king, albeit at times a child, a very weak leader or the catalyst for civil war.

Development (pages 152–169)

The brief stories on pages 152–153 provide evidence of royal power at three different periods. Pupils use these to hypothesise about the shape of the Royal Rollercoaster from Henry VIII to George IV.

The power factors for the Activity on page 153 should probably be something like this:

1. 15 November 1539, the story of Richard Whiting, Abbot of Glastonbury – Henry VIII was king: power factor of about 9/10 (pupils may give him 10/10 because there is nothing in the story to suggest any limit to his authority).

2. 30 January 1649, the story of Charles I's execution: power factor of perhaps 0–1/10. Charles clearly had some sympathisers among the crowd but the sympathy does not give him much power and having no head is about as powerless as you can get!

3. April 1827, the story of George IV. He had some power – a 'few important decisions' still rested with the King – but he was not interested in exercising it: 3–5/10.

So the hypothetical Royal Rollercoaster will start high in the 1500s and continue there until it drops dramatically at 1649 and then rises again to flatten out somewhere below the mid-point by 1827. Pupils' sketches are likely to be similar to that on pages 154–155. To answer question 2b) on page 155, they should realise they need more information before they can identify 'mistakes'.

Put your ruler in the Hot Seat! (pages 156–169)
This Activity (page 156) should be completed within a lesson, though some preparation (see below) could be done beforehand.
The important points are:
For teachers
- Have extra resources to hand – this could have been given as a homework task or be part of a library lesson. Teaching pupils how to use ICT effectively, so that they are not copying and pasting huge chunks of incomprehensible text, is very important but should be done in advance of this activity or the pace will be lost.
- Draw attention to the different elements of the brief (page 157)
- Give time limits: for example, 20 minutes research; 5 minutes to design the rollercoaster; 5 minutes to decide who will do what in the presentation, to draw any pictures or diagrams and to gather props
- If possible, have a few props available.
For pupils
- Selection of relevant information is the key skill – more is NOT better
- Every member of the group must have a task and participate in some way in the presentation (explaining, acting or miming a scene, holding up pictures, diagrams or the section of the Rollercoaster, etc.)
- Read the instructions carefully (page 157)
- Be aware of time limits – both for research and for the presentation.

Plenary

Why were ideas and attitudes to monarchy changing? (pages 170–171)
Question 1: ideas about monarchy
It is easy to see how ideas about the king or queen and religion and war have changed. The other ideas do not match up so easily. Pupils are only asked to explain one example but should also have an overview of how power has transferred from monarch to Parliament. The table overleaf summarises the changes.
Question 2: The factor that suggests **when** the power of the monarchy changed is religion.
Question 3: Charles I's execution proved that there were alternatives to having a king. The power of the king and style of government had to change if the monarch was ill or lazy. Increasing wealth, population and technology changed communication.

Assessment for Learning – Outcomes to look for

a) Can pupils explain some of the things about the role of the monarchy since 1500 that have changed?
b) Can pupils give some examples of particular changes and say when they took place (context or date)?
c) Can pupils suggest some reasons for the changes?

This table summarises the changes in the power of the monarchy in response to the Activity on page 170.

	Middle Ages	1800s
War	The king is expected to lead his army in war, using well-organised and well-planned tactics	War is planned by officials and led by generals
Religion	Kings are chosen by God, so rebelling against the king is challenging God	Parliament has decided that the monarch must be Protestant. He is not chosen by God
Bad kings	Bad kings don't listen to advice. This has caused quarrels and even led to some kings being replaced	Monarchs who are too lazy or sick to rule have just increased Parliament's power
Ruling the country	Parliament agrees taxation, usually to pay for the king's wars; it meets when the king calls it and ends when the king dismisses it Having a king is the only way a country can be ruled A king's job is to defend his people and keep law and order but he doesn't need to be involved in decisions about daily life	Parliament is in control. The Prime Minister can manage without the monarch if he has the support of Parliament The Prime Minister leads the government. He can be changed if he doesn't do a good job With all the changes in society – new towns, jobs, machines, etc. – a team of people is needed to make decisions about all aspects of ruling the country. This team should be elected

Hero or villain? Why do reputations change over time?

Summary	This short enquiry looks at why attitudes to Cromwell have changed since his death. Doing History is about change and continuity and the Big Story summarises the changes in royal power between Henry VIII and Queen Victoria.
Time needed	1–2 hours
Key concepts and processes	**Interpretation:** Cromwell, hero or monster? **Change and continuity:** King v. Parliament
Resources	• Pupil's Book pages 172–177 • Activity sheet 40

↕ Objectives

By the end of this enquiry pupils should:
- know that attitudes towards Oliver Cromwell have changed several times since his death and be able to give examples of those changes
- recognise that the events and experiences of people at different periods influence attitudes towards Cromwell
- be able to suggest reasons why there are disagreements about Oliver Cromwell and his role in history
- understand what is meant by a 'turning point' and be able to give an example
- be able to recognise and exemplify both changes and things that did not change a great deal in the big story of monarchy.

↕ Lesson sequence

Starter (pages 172–173)

1. The four statements match with the time periods as follows:
B – Charles II's reign: (thumbs down):
- Cromwell was involved in regicide of Charles I
- Charles II and most English people wanted to end all reminders of Puritan rule
- People wanted to discredit Cromwell.

A – The Victorian period (thumbs up):
- People wanted to celebrate parliamentary democracy
- People were proud of British soldiers like Cromwell
- Many people at that time were very religious like Cromwell
- They also disapproved of drinking and gambling.

D – The 1930s and 40s (thumbs down):
- Hitler was a dictator with some similarities to Cromwell.

C – Today (thumb half up/half down):
- Historians try to be balanced in their assessment
- People recognise good and bad in Cromwell.

See also Activity sheet 40.

2. The graph should show the steep up and down in Cromwell's reputation, ending with a rise to today's mid-point.
3. The graph can be annotated as above.
4. The publication of Cromwell's letters and speeches has allowed fairer interpretations of the man and his actions.
5. The Irish, in particular, cannot forgive his intolerance towards Catholics and the way his army massacred the people of Drogheda and Wexford.

Doing History: Change and continuity (pages 174–175)

Year 7 ideas about change and continuity are revised through analysis of the four speech bubbles given here.

1. *Changed:* the relative power of monarch and Parliament between 1530s and 1770
2. *Stayed the same:* the monarch can still exercise considerable power in 1770
3. *Quickest change:* Charles I's execution
4. *Slowest change:* development in power of Parliament
5. *Turning point:* the execution – 'England will never be the same again.'
6. *Other possible turning points:* Henry VIII's divorce led to changes in religion; dissolution of the monasteries caused significant social changes; the new Elizabethan Poor Law also changed social practice; the appointment of the first Prime Minister by George I recognised a change in government.

Learning Log (page 175)

The points above summarise what pupils need to record in their own words, with an example or brief explanation for each one.

The Big Story: Power Part Two – monarchy (pages 176–177)

To end, focus on the overall Royal Rollercoaster. Pupils should make sure their own version is complete and annotated.

The questions give the teacher an opportunity to differentiate, asking for factual information from weaker pupils and higher order analysis from the most able.

The rollercoaster should guide pupils but there are no right answers.

Learning Log (page 177)

This will be the completed rollercoaster from the previous lesson sequence – it could be photocopied and reduced in size if individual members of the group need their own.

◆) Assessment for Learning – Outcomes to look for

a) Can pupils give examples of ways in which attitudes to Oliver Cromwell have changed over time?

b) Can pupils give an example of an event or experience from the past that has influenced how people have felt about Cromwell?

c) Can pupils explain one or more reasons why attitudes towards Cromwell have been different at different periods in history?

d) Are pupils able to describe what is meant by a 'turning point' in history and suggest examples?

e) Can pupils give examples of changes in the monarchy and things that did not change between 1500 and 1900?

SECTION 6 OVERVIEW
POWER: DEMOCRACY: HOW DID ORDINARY PEOPLE WIN THE RIGHT TO VOTE?

This section concentrates on the power of the people, as opposed to the monarchy, and the demand for the vote, that grew from the late eighteenth century. Pupils decide whether it is more effective to bring about reform through violent or non-violent action, looking at the consequences of campaigns for change in the eighteenth and nineteenth centuries. They have to present their conclusions in a powerful and convincing speech.

Lesson sequence 14: How can you change things for the better? (pp. 178–193)

A look at the aims and motivations of different groups of revolutionaries in eighteenth-century France, the consequences of the Revolution and the advantages and disadvantages of peaceful protest or violence.

Lesson sequence 15: Winning the vote in nineteenth century Britain (pp. 194–203)

What were the consequences of attempts to extend the vote to ordinary people at Peterloo?

Lesson sequence 16: How did the Chartists try to win the vote? (pp. 204–215)

The story of the Chartists and their efforts to improve the electoral system and extend the franchise in nineteenth-century Britain.

How can you change things for the better?

Summary	This lesson sequence introduces ideas about violent and non-violent campaigns for reform which will be the focus of a speech which is the challenge for the whole section. The content details the events and outcomes of the French Revolution, seen from the point of view of three eye-witnesses, representing different classes of French society.
Time needed	3 hours
Key concepts and processes	**Cause and consequence:** making explanatory links **Communicating about the past:** develop speaking skills, organising information accurately in a structured and substantiated explanation
Resources	• Pupil's Book pages 178–193 • Activity sheets 41–45

Objectives

By the end of this enquiry pupils should be able to:
- research and record the aims, methods and outcomes of different participants in the French Revolution
- explain some of the consequences of the French Revolution and make links between them
- organise information so they have a clear structure for presenting their opinions
- use appropriate language and terminology for the task.

Lesson sequence

Starter (pages 178–179)

These two pages about the American Declaration of Independence are important because pupils:
- are reminded that life for many ordinary people was hard and unfair and they had no legal way of bringing about changes and improvements
- need to understand that paying taxes is accepted as a part of citizenship but people resent having no say in how much, how often and what the money is used for

- must recognise what a tremendous challenge the Declaration of Independence was to the views of society and government held by most people at that time.

Discuss
Question 1 – The Declaration of Independence challenges the five 'Before' statements as follows:
1. People are not equal – *All men are created equal ...*
2. Ordinary people do not have any rights – *They are given certain Rights by their Creator ... Among these are Life, Liberty and the pursuit of Happiness*
3. Kings get their power direct from God – *Governments are set up ... gaining their power from the agreement of the governed*
4. The upper classes run the government because they own lots of land – *Governments are set up ... gaining their power from the agreement of the governed* (the right to govern does not come from having land or wealth)
5. Rebellion is a sin and a 'treason', which is the worst form of crime – *whenever any Form of Government becomes destructive of these ends, it is the Right of the People to alter or to abolish it, and set up a new Government.*
See also Activity sheet 41.

Development (pages 180–207)

How can you change things for the better?
The major enquiry into the development of democracy culminates in pupils making a speech, using information from three lesson sequences, the first being about the French Revolution.

- It is important that pupils keep track of what they learn.
- Key points could be summarised at the end of each lesson or research period and displayed on a large poster or saved on an interactive whiteboard.
- Pupils could do the research in pairs but one should support James' view and one support Sarah's when it comes to the final speech. This will be challenging for any pupil who has to argue against their own personal opinion but they should be able to find enough evidence to support either case.

- To link the three case studies it might be useful to have the focus of the speech on display for regular reference:
  'The best way to win the vote is by …'

What did the French Revolution achieve? (pages 182–193)
Why were the French angry?
After reading the information about the organisation of French society pupils may find it helpful to use Activity sheet 42 to remind them of the structure of society in France on the eve of the revolution.

The Revolution begins (pages 184–185)
Every pupil should create two versions of the Revolution Chart (Activity sheet 43), the first covering the period 1786–1791 and the second covering the period 1791–1815, which they will complete as they work through the enquiry. From the information on page 183, pupils should be able to complete the aims as below.

Revolution Chart: 1786–1791			
	Aims What did they want?	**Methods** Did they use peaceful or violent methods to achieve their aims?	**Outcomes** What were the consequences? Did s/he get what s/he wanted?
Henri, the bourgeois	To be able to vote To worship freely		
Edith, the sans-culottes	To have higher wages To stop rents and bread prices rising To end starvation		
Gaston, the peasant	To pay less tax and rent To stop bread prices rising To end starvation		

Section 6

Stage 1: The bourgeois revolution (page 184)
Pupils complete the methods and outcomes columns of their chart for Henri at this stage. Pupils now need to work through Stages 2 and 3 and the Declaration of the Rights of Man (pages 186–187) in the same way.

After reading and discussing the events of 1789 pupils complete the methods and outcomes columns on their Revolution Charts.
The answer to Activity question 2 on page 186 is that, by August 1789, the bourgeoisie had achieved what they wanted. The sans-culottes and peasants had not.

Revolution Chart: 1786–1791			
	Aims What did they want?	**Methods** Did they use peaceful or violent methods to achieve their aims?	**Outcomes** What were the consequences? Did s/he get what s/he wanted?
Henri, the bourgeois	To be able to vote To worship freely	Ignored First and Second Estates Took Tennis Court Oath Peaceful action	Set up the National Assembly Abolished several taxes Ended the King's right to imprison people without trial Planned new, more democratic constitution Declaration of the Rights of Man
Edith, the sans-culottes	To have higher wages To stop rents and bread prices rising To end starvation	Broke into warehouses for grain and weapons Stormed the Bastille and killed the governor Took charge of the king Violent action	Declaration of the Rights of Man gave equality in law and freedom of worship. Tax was fairer These were not the main concerns of the sans-culottes and they were still hungry
Gaston, the peasant	To pay less tax and rent To stop bread prices rising To end starvation	Attacked barns and chateaux belonging to nobles and Church Violent action	The Great Fear led to the nobility and Churchmen renouncing all privileges Declaration of the Rights of Man gave equality in law and freedom of worship. Tax was fairer These were not the main concerns of the peasants and they were still hungry

The Execution of the King: January 1793 (page 188)

The second version of the Revolution Chart, Activity sheet 43, should look something like this:

Revolution Chart: 1791–1815			
	Aims What did they want?	**Methods** Did they use peaceful or violent methods to achieve their aims?	**Outcomes** What were the consequences? Did s/he get what s/he wanted?
Henri, the bourgeois	To keep the National Assembly as it was, so being able to vote and worship freely	Unable to do anything	War with Europe Business ruined Lived in fear
Edith, the sans-culottes	To rule France To have higher wages To stop rents and bread prices rising To end starvation	Execution of the king and members of First and Second Estates Took control of Paris Slogans and revolutionary 'tricolour' 'Direct democracy' – got rid of anyone who did not carry out their wishes Violent action	Ruled France through establishment of the Committee of Public Safety Fixed bread price
Gaston, the peasant	To stop the war To pay less tax and rent To stop bread prices rising To end starvation	Rebellion in the Vendée Violent action	Hated the Terror Were paid less for the food they grew Rebellion put down by sans-culottes government by murder, rape and burning of crops

The Terror: 1792–1794 (page 189)

Discussion

1. During 1792–1794 the sans-culottes were in control and had achieved their aims. Henri, having had a taste of success but also living in fear that he could be the next victim, must have been the most unhappy at this time.

The peasants were mostly left alone, unless they rebelled, and had never really come near to having their concerns addressed.

2. Pupils could use two different highlighters to select evidence for their speeches from the Revolution Charts.

The Emperor Napoleon/What did the Revolution do for me? (pages 190–191)
Final details that could be added to the Revolution Charts:
Henri: never used violence
Outcomes
• opportunity to buy more land
• education and new careers
• the vote
• control of the National Assembly for nineteenth century.
Edith
Outcomes
• lost power in 1795
• return to poverty and hunger
• no longer helped by the Church.
Gaston
Outcomes
• rents increased but paid less tax
• opportunity to buy some land
• right to vote because of being small landowner.
Pupils should conclude from this that:
• extremes of violence did bring about change
• a high level of bloodshed could not be sustained
• in the long term those who used peaceful negotiation came out best
• peaceful protest may not have achieved much without the threat of violence and support from violent revolutionaries, forcing those in power to change.
The two charts must be kept until the other case studies are completed.

Plenary

Consequences of the French Revolution (pages 192–193)
Activity 1
The Power-ometer (see Activity sheet 44) could be a large-scale display on the classroom wall in the same way a giant thermometer is used when fund-raising. Pointers should be added to the diagram as each stage of the Revolution is studied. It serves as an overview of events and can be used as a quick, mini-plenary '...so, where are we now?' As such it would be helpful to include the brief descriptions a)–g), page 192, on the pointers, as well as the dates.
The date box is only needed if you can create a moving Power-ometer arrow and rolling dates for the date window.
• The pointer for a) has already been drawn but needs to be labelled

• Pointer b) should show the nobles were in control in 1788 because Louis had agreed to negotiate with them through the Estates General, where the First and Second Estates could outvote the rest
• Pointer c) should show the bourgeoisie had taken the lead in 1789, by ignoring the Estates General and demanding increased democracy
• Pointer d) should show the sans-culottes are in control
• Pointer e) is the peasants' moment of supremacy
• Pointer f) should show control moving back to the sans-culottes for a second time
• Pointer g) should show that, when Napoleon was Emperor (or 'King'), power rested with him, despite the bourgeoisie benefitting from many aspects of the Code Napoleon.

Activity 2 (page 192)
1. Sort the cards into causes and consequences. See Activity sheet 45.
Causes:
• Louis XVI did not have enough money to run France
• Many French people lived in great poverty
• The American Declaration of Independence gave other countries a thirst for liberty.
All other cards are consequences.
2. Spread out the consequence cards on a large sheet of paper and draw lines to show how they can link up. It is possible to make 'chains of events' or a spider diagram with multiple links. For example:
a) The meeting of the Estates General ⟶ National Assembly ⟶ nobles lose power ⟶ Declaration of Rights of Man ⟶ revolutionary ideas spread ⟶ other governments cracked down on protest ⟶ France was at war ⟶ peasants rebelled.
b) During the Terror, thousands were executed ⟶ nobles lost power ⟶ many sans-culottes were better off ⟶ poor in other countries were inspired to protest.
c) During the Terror, thousands were executed ⟶ the King and Queen were executed ⟶ France became a republic ⟶ Napoleon crowned himself Emperor.
There are many variations and additional links. Some of the links are really clear but some, like war following increase in protest or Napoleon following on from the French republic, are more tenuous.

Activity 3 (page 193)
Before moving on from the French Revolution, pupils must note down at least two points that they will use for their speeches.

⬍⟩ **Assessment for Learning – Outcomes to look for**

a) Have pupils recorded the aims, methods and outcomes of different participants in the French Revolution in the two Revolution Charts?

b) Can they explain some of the consequences of the French Revolution and make links between them?

c) Can they give examples of points about the advantages and disadvantages of violent or non-violent action that they will use in their final speech?

d) Are they able to use key terms from the lesson sequence correctly, e.g. bourgeois?

Winning the vote in nineteenth-century Britain

Summary	This enquiry looks at the attempts in the first half of the nineteenth century to give ordinary British people a political voice, so they could improve their living and working conditions. The 'Peterloo Massacre' and the campaign of 1832 are case studies providing more evidence for the speech about the best methods for achieving reform.
Time needed	About 3 hours, possibly less
Key concepts and processes	**Cause and consequence:** consider the impact of violence on the rate of reform
Resources	• Pupil's Book pages 194–203 • Activity sheets 46, 47A–B

Objectives

By the end of this enquiry pupils should be able to:
- explain aspects of living and working conditions for ordinary people in Britain in the early nineteenth century
- describe problems with the British voting system in the early nineteenth century
- give examples of protests against the voting system and explain their outcomes
- assess whether the use of violence helped or hindered the cause.

Lesson sequence

Starter (pages 194–195)

What did the government see?
For the Activity on page 195, to produce a memo to the Prime Minister, pupils should rewrite Source 1 in their own words, adding comments about the implications for Britain. As a memo it could start with 'Sir ...' or 'To The Right Honourable Mr William Pitt' or simply 'Dear Prime Minister, ...'
The memo should mention:
- the horrors occurring in France – something to worry about

- the poor in France were attracted by revolutionary ideas – there are poor people in England
- the murder of Louis XVI, resulting from violence getting out of control – the PM himself could be in danger (see also the headlines, page 194)
- the potential damage done to trade and property as a result of revolution and how important these are for Britain
- even religion can be a victim of revolutionary ideas and actions
- revolutionary ideas are being spread in pamphlets and similar papers and it is essential to stop their circulation.

See also Activity sheet 46.

Development (pages 196–201)

Why did ordinary people want change? (pages 196–197)
This enquiry is designed to provide an overview of the circumstances and events that led to Chartism, the major reform movement of the nineteenth century.
The main areas of complaint were:
Working conditions
- Machinery – dangerous; created dirty, dusty air; non-stop
- Hours

- Jobs – plenty of workers, so like it or lump it; harsh punishments for small offences; could be laid off.

Living conditions
- Poor, overcrowded housing
- Poor sanitation and waste disposal
- Polluted air and water.

Short-term problems
- Unemployment after the war
- New machinery took jobs
- Food prices
- Taxation.

What was wrong with British elections? (pages 198–199)
For question 1 of the Activity on page 198, pupils should be able to list the following

problems.
- Only rich people could be MPs
- All counties sent two MPs to Parliament, regardless of their size or population
- New industrial towns didn't have any representation at all
- 'Rotten Boroughs' meant that in some places MPs were elected by hardly any voters
- When people voted they had to declare their choice in public
- It was easy to bribe people to support a particular candidate

For question 2, any two problems could be chosen to complete their table. The table below shows some ideas for this task. Activity sheet 47A provides a blank table for them to fill in.

Major problems	How it should be changed*	Why the government might oppose this
Very few men were allowed to vote and no women	Everyone over a certain age allowed to vote so that laws are passed that will help the poor	Fear of revolutionary ideas Old system has worked for a long time
Only rich people could be MPs	Allow anyone to become an MP	The rich benefit from the country doing well so they will always make the best decisions for Britain
All counties sent two MPs to Parliament, regardless of their size or population	The number of MPs representing each area should depend on the number of people living there	
New industrial towns didn't have any representation at all	Towns and cities should be represented in the same way as any other area, according to population	There are potentially more troublemakers in towns and cities – they should not have a chance to vote or they might choose a revolutionary candidate
'Rotten Boroughs' meant that in some places MPs were elected by hardly any voters	Scrap all Rotten Boroughs and include them in the surrounding area	MPs who were elected for Rotten Boroughs might lose their parliamentary seats
When people voted they had to declare their choice in public	Make all ballots secret to prevent threats and bribery	Rich MPs would have no control over the voting and might lose their parliamentary seats
It was easy to bribe people to support a particular candidate	Make all ballots secret to prevent bribery Put a limit on how much can be spent trying to get support	

*The suggestions in this column are based on liberal 21st-century thinking – pupils may not all agree.

Peterloo 1819: what did they want and did they get it? (pages 200–201)
The story of St Peter's Fields could be retold as a newspaper report. It would be an excellent opportunity to try particular journalistic styles and write from the perspective of one of the participants – a demonstrator or one of the Yeomanry – or of the government. Alternatively, it could be, anachronistically, a radio or television news report, including interviews with several interested parties.
For question 1 of the Activity, columns 2–4 of the chart could be completed as follows.
See also Activity sheet 47B.

	Aims What did the protestors want?	Actions Did they use peaceful or violent methods to achieve their aims?	Outcomes What were the consequences of what they did? Did they get what they wanted?	Lessons from history What evidence could James or Sarah use in their speeches?
Peterloo protesters 1819	Reform of Parliament Reduction of taxes Votes for all adults	Meeting called Non-violent protest march Protest turned violent because magistrates called in the Yeomanry	11 dead, 400 injured Meetings of more than 50 people banned Magistrates increase powers Newspaper tax increased to make them too expensive for ordinary workers No change in right to vote	

Question 2: The government chose option b) largely because of fear of revolution. Events in France were still very recent. They had started with demands for reform and spread through publication of pamphlets etc. urging protest. Also, many MPs had a vested interest in maintaining the status quo, as outlined in reasons why the government might oppose reform of the voting system, above.
Question 3: Pupils should remember the context before condemning the magistrates out of hand. Think of the events mentioned in the headlines on page 194 – fear of revolution was very real.
Question 4: Evidence for James and Sarah:
• crowds of people can be seen as a threat, even if that is not the intention
• peaceful protest can very easily be crushed
• in the end, whatever the intention, violence can make the authorities even more scared and then they react more strongly.

Plenary

The reform riots of 1831: the same story?
(pages 202–203)

Use Activity sheet 47B. The extra row of the table should look something like this:

	Aims What did the protestors want?	Actions Did they use peaceful or violent methods to achieve their aims?	Outcomes What were the consequences of what they did? Did they get what they wanted?	Lessons from history What evidence could James or Sarah use in their speeches?
Reform riots of 1831	Changes to the voting system so that ordinary people had a say in how the country was run	Violent riots in Nottingham – attack on Nottingham castle	Rioters arrested – three executed, six transported Violent riots in Bristol – set fire to important buildings, property destroyed, people killed Threat of march on London which soldiers refused to stop The Reform Act – extending the vote to more men but still only 20% and they had to have property; new industrial cities had MPs	

Question 3a): Any discussion should include the following points:
- great majority of population still not allowed to vote
- voting was still a public declaration
- the balance between north and south/urban and rural was still unfair.

Question 3b): Again the context is important:
- MPs were changing a system that had been in place for a long time and were unlikely to want to sweep away all the traditional practices over night
- without violence there may have been no changes – the first attempt to pass a Reform Bill had been rejected
- new MPs were pushing for change from the inside but some may have been scared off by the violence.

Question 4: Evidence for James and Sarah:
- violence successfully precipitated some reform
- that reform may have been limited by fear of violence
- reform may have happened anyway.

Assessment for Learning – Outcomes to look for

a) Can pupils explain aspects of living and working conditions for ordinary people in the early nineteenth century, giving examples?

b) Can pupils describe several problems with the British voting system in the early nineteenth century?

c) Can pupils describe some of the causes and events of the St Peter's Fields protest and explain their outcomes?

d) Have pupils made relevant contributions to discussion about whether the use of violence helped or hindered the cause of reform?

e) Have pupils been able to fill in the final column of their chart without much support?

Linked web-based activities

Pre-1832 election game
http://www.thinkinghistory.co.uk/ActivityBase/Pre1832ElectionGame.html

Plan for lesson sequence 16	How did the Chartists try to win the vote?
Summary	This enquiry describes the Chartist campaign to win the vote for working men. It draws together all the information needed to write the speech about the most successful methods of protest and provides the Double Hamburger model for structuring an argument. Doing History is about consequences and the sequence finishes by tying up the loose ends of the nineteenth century story of electoral reform.
Time needed	3 hours – most activities are short but time will be required to prepare and deliver the speeches
Key concepts and processes	**Consequences:** short and long term; intended or unintended, so unpredictable **Communicating about the past:** develop speaking skills; organising information accurately in a structured and substantiated explanation
Resources	• Pupil's Book pages 204–215 • Activity sheet 47B

Objectives

By the end of this enquiry pupils should be able to:
- understand and exemplify that there are many consequences of events and actions
- explain and give examples of different kinds of consequences, such as short and long term or intended and unintended
- organise information so they have a clear structure for presenting their opinions
- use appropriate language and terminology for the task.

Lesson sequence

Starter (pages 204–205)

An introduction to the Charter and the Chartists
The summary of the six points of the Charter should be in the pupils' own words to ensure good understanding.

For example:
1. All men to be allowed to vote unless they are mad or criminal.
2. People should be able to keep their votes secret.
3. Allow any man to become an MP whether he is rich or poor.
4. Start paying MPs so ordinary working men can give up their jobs to look after their constituency.
5. The number of MPs for any area should be decided by the number of people who can vote.
6. Hold elections for Parliament every year so that corrupt MPs cannot afford annual payment of bribes and poor MPs can be replaced.

Development

Use Activity sheet 47B again. The new row of the table for Activity 2 (page 205) should look something like this:

	Aims What did the protestors want?	**Actions** Did they use peaceful or violent methods to achieve their aims?	**Outcomes** What were the consequences of what they did? Did they get what they wanted?	**Lessons from history** What evidence could James or Sarah use in their speeches?
The Chartists	The six points of the People's Charter	Two groups: 'Moral Force' – meetings, letters, education, wanted to show they were honest, sober, deserving 'Physical Force' – large meetings, passionate speeches using language that encouraged violence	Three presentations of petition to House of Commons rejected by large majorities Strikes organised in support of the Charter – ending in violence as government sends in soldiers Peaceful demonstration of thousands of Chartists in London – petition taken to Parliament Vote not given to working men	Despite trying both tactics the Chartists weren't successful The government was not scared of the protestors – it was more frightened of allowing working people the vote

1848 – the Chartist Revolution? (page 207)
Thinking for the Activity should take the following into account:
- the papers read by government officials would focus on
  - how the Queen and key buildings were saved from potential danger
  - how London was properly protected – special constables appointed; soldiers and police on standby; cannons in place
  - the potential threat of so many with radical ideas being stirred by inflammatory speeches

- papers read by working men would focus on
  - a very large crowd turned up to hear the speeches
  - those who stayed to hear the speeches despite the pouring rain
  - the fact that huge numbers of police and soldiers were unnecessary because the event was peaceful
  - the thousands who signed the petition which was successfully delivered to Parliament.

What is the best way to win the vote? (pages 208–209)

Planning your speech

The Double Hamburger provides a very structured and detailed frame for the big speech. Pupils can work in pairs, taking opposite sides and trying out different arguments on each other. Speeches could be recorded or spoken to a small group rather than delivered to the whole class.

For this task pupils must:

- decide whether they are taking James' or Sarah's view – they cannot opt for 'a bit of both'
- prepare an individual speech
- use the examples they have recorded on their charts as evidence.

The arguments from page 209 should be divided as follows:

Sarah – 2; 3; 6; 7; James – 1; 4; 5; 8.

Pupils should also look at pages 210–211.

Doing History: Consequences (pages 210–211)

This provides examples of three different statements about Consequences from Section 6. Pupils should use the three British events summarised on page 211 to find another example for each statement.

A single event or decision can have many different consequences

- Both Peterloo and the Reform Riots had several consequences
- Drawing up the People's Charter had many consequences

Consequences can be of different kinds, for example short term

- The speakers at Peterloo were put in prison
- Buildings were destroyed
- Punishments, including execution and transportation, were handed out to violent demonstrators

… and long-term consequences

- The government was frightened that if they gave in this would only encourage more violence
- Middle-class men were given the vote after the Reform Riots

Some consequences are intended

- Middle-class men were given the vote after the Reform Riots
- Chartist groups were set up all over the country
- Working-class people became interested in politics

- Millions of people signed the Chartist petition

… some are unintended and so cannot be predicted

- At Peterloo, 11 people were killed and many wounded
- Many chartist miners were killed in Newport
- The government banned meetings of more than 50 people
- Working people felt betrayed after 1831 and were more determined to win the vote.

Learning Log

The ideas about consequences would make a good mind map.

So who was proved right? (page 212)

Listening to men in the MPs' club, James and Sarah would probably have to conclude that both were actually right in part – that both forms of protest had some impact.

James was right that

- peaceful protest only brought change slowly
- violence brought the issues to public attention
- fear of violence started the process of reform.

He was wrong that

- violence would bring about change quickly – in Britain it made MPs even more frightened of giving working people the vote.

Sarah was right that

- violence led to imprisonment, suffering and even death
- governments do not want to appear weak and therefore do not give into violence
- intelligence, education and peaceful protest impress MPs.

But wrong that

- everyone could get what they wanted by proving they were responsible citizens – it wasn't until 1884 that most men were allowed to vote and women had to wait until 1918.

In the MPs' club, both would have to admit that by 1867 the context had changed and it had been a long while since there was a real threat of revolution.

What were the consequences? (page 213)

The timeline should lead to some discussion that may help young people to understand the importance of the right to vote and access to education.

Pupils should decide their own Golden Rules but might include:

- Don't expect reform overnight – especially if what you want to change has been in place a long time.

- Get lots of people on your side, including those who hold power, if possible.
- Show you are not a threat but deserve to achieve the aim of the campaign.
- Make a lot of noise to show you are determined – but actual violence may be counter-productive.

Plenary

The Big Story: Power Part Two – democracy (pages 214–215)
Learning Log
Pupils should use the timeline of ideas and attitudes of the rulers and government (above the timeline) and ideas and attitudes of ordinary working people (below the timeline) to answer the questions on page 215. Answers to question 1 are: a) no; b) yes; c) no; d) no.

Assessment for Learning – Outcomes to look for

a) Can pupils give examples of some of the consequences of Peterloo, the Reform Riots or Chartism?
b) Can pupils explain different kinds of consequences such as short and long term or intended and unintended and suggest some examples?
c) Did pupils use the Double Hamburger structure successfully to organise information for their speech?
d) Did they explain their opinions clearly and support points with evidence?
e) Did they include some subject specific terms and use an appropriate tone and language for the task?

Linked web-based activities

Shall we join the Chartists?
http://www.thinkinghistory.co.uk/ActivityBase/ShallWeJoinChartists.html

CONCLUSION
WHAT HAVE YOU LEARNED THIS YEAR?

This section requires pupils to reflect on
what they have learnt during the year, asking
them to join up their thinking by linking
different elements and to select what was,
for them, most memorable. It also gives a
glimpse at the topics to come in Year 9.

What have you learned this year?

Summary	The conclusion summarises the learning points from the book – about sources; significance; the key people; the Big Stories; ideas and beliefs. Building the History Wall links the content topics and enquiry questions with the concepts and processes. The final task refers back to the start of the book, asking pupils to think of an engaging and descriptive title.
Time needed	2 hours
Key concepts and processes	Summary of several
Resources	• Pupil's Book pages 216–228 • Activity sheets 48–50

Objectives

By the end of this lesson sequence pupils should be able to:
- categorise sources
- select significant events and people from the period 1500–1900
- explain, or start to describe, the criteria they have used to make their selection of significant events and people
- make links between the themes and topics they have studied

- summarise some of the changes in ideas and attitudes over time
- draw up a list of good historical questions.

Lesson sequence

Starter (pages 216–217)

... about sources?
See Activity sheet 48. The completed table should look like this:

	Surviving buildings	Objects	Pictures	Writing	Photographs
'Early Modern period' 1500–1750	A	F	D	E	
'Industrial period' 1750–1900		C G	F		B H
Source not available until after 1900 I, J					

Development

... about significance: what and who should be remembered? (pages 218–221)

The activity for recapping significance is self-explanatory but attention should be drawn to the Doing History recap box, which reminds pupils that it is not the same as being famous. They may need to refer back to earlier work (Section 4, page 135) to look at criteria.

Question 1:

Christine Counsell has described an event/development as significant if it is/has:

- *Remarkable* – it was remarked upon by people at the time and/or since
- *Remembered* – it was important at some stage in history within the collective memory of a group or groups
- *Resulted in change* – it had consequences for the future
- *Resonant* – people like to make analogies with it; it is possible to connect with experiences, beliefs or situations across time and space
- *Revealing* – of some other aspect of the past.

But a higher level of challenge is for pupils to develop their own criteria and argue in defence of their own perspective. To make selection for the Activity easier, Activity sheet 49 has all the stamps on one page for pupils to annotate, cross out etc. Pupils can work from memory to decide which people were significant in the period 1500–1900 or they can use pages 219–221.

To provide a starting point, Ian Dawson has suggested that reasons for a person being significant could be if s/he:

- changed events at the time they lived
- improved lots of people's lives – or made them worse
- changed people's ideas
- had a long-lasting impact on their country or the world
- had been a really good or a very bad example to other people of how to live or behave.

But again, pupils should be making their choices using their own criteria, if possible.

Question 2:

A good homework task might be to create a poster advertising the choice of national holiday. The poster would need to suggest why the person/event was significant.

Activity (page 221), Question 1

The groups of people are:

Imperialists: Edward I; Cortes; Rhodes
Involved in the campaign to end the slave trade: William Wilberforce; Toussaint L'Ouverture; Olaudah Equiano; Thomas Clarkson
Victims of a king's power: Robert Aske; Richard Whiting; John Pym
Politicians who wanted reform: Thomas Jefferson; Henry Hunt; Robespierre
Involved in attempted invasions of England: Nelson; Napoleon; Philip II of Spain; Francis Drake
British rulers: Henry VIII; Elizabeth I; Charles I; Oliver Cromwell
Inventors: James Watt; Michael Faraday; Isambard Kingdom Brunel
Ordinary men who became involved in dramatic events: a Peterloo casualty; a Civil War soldier; a sans-culottes; a Pilgrim Father.

Question 2: Pupils should work in pairs or small groups for this and, together, draw up a list of questions to ask. It would be worth discussing the need to ask open questions in an interview. The best questions will be reasonably specific; for example, asking a Civil War soldier

What was your opinion of King Charles?
Will you describe what it was like at his execution?

would be better than

What was life like?

... about Big Stories: can you make connections? (pages 222–223)

This Active Learning task works best in a fairly large open space.

Activity sheet 50 can be used to record the links but it is fun to have the photographs as well!

... about ideas and beliefs? (pages 224–225)

Into the mind of ...

Answers to question 1:

- thoughts of people from the 1300s (the Middle Ages): A, C, H, L
- thoughts of people from the 1500s and 1600s: A, F, G, H
- thoughts of people from the 1800s: B, D, E, I, J, K, M.

Ideas C and L would be especially important in the Middle Ages.
Ideas F and G were new in the 1500s and 1600s.
Ideas B, D and M were important in the 1800s, and new means of transport I and J had an impact on everyday life and attitudes to travel, holidays, etc.

Conclusion

Coming soon in the Big Story of ... (pages 226–227)

Questions should consider:

- Diversity, for example:
  Why were ... experiences different from ...?
  How should we record the lives of ...?
- Change and continuity, for example:
  What changed in the story of ... between ... and ...
  What similarities can be seen in the events of ... and ...?
  Why might ... be considered a turning point?
- Cause and consequence, for example:
  Why did ... happen?
  What were the consequences of ...?
  How many causes can you think of for ... and how are connected?
  How can the results of ... be linked?
- Significance, for example:
  Why should ... be remembered?
  How should we decide if ... was significant?
- Interpretation, for example:
  Why do ... and ... disagree about ...?
  What does ... tell us about ... ideas?

Plenary

The book with no name! (page 228)

This really has to be done using ICT, giving access to images and fonts etc. and the cover template. It should be an enjoyable way for pupils to reflect on what has really stuck out from the Year 8 course.

♦⟩ Assessment for Learning – Outcomes to look for

Each mini-activity will provide evidence of what the pupils have learnt. Outcomes will show they have:

- successfully categorised sources
- selected significant events and people from the period 1500–1900
- described, or perhaps explained, the criteria they have used to make their selection of significant events and people
- made links between the themes and topics they have studied, shown by their photographs or diagrams
- summarised some of the changes in ideas and attitudes over time
- drawn up a list of good historical questions.

And, hopefully, had fun and enjoyed studying history!

PROGRESSION IN KEY CONCEPTS FROM YEAR 7 TO YEAR 8

	Year 7 Key Points	Year 8 Progression
Causes	Most events have a number of causes. Even if there are lots of causes there's usually one that finally sets off an event. Causes are not equally important.	Causes of an event are often linked.
Consequences	A single event or decision can have many different consequences.	Consequences can be of different kinds, for example short and long term consequences. Some consequences are intended, some are unintended and so cannot be predicted.
Change and continuity	At any one time there are things that are changing and things that are staying the same. Some changes happen quickly. Some happen slowly.	A key change in a pattern of events is often called a turning point. A turning point is a time of great change, leaving things permanently different from how they were before.
Significance	Being significant is not the same as being famous. Events are significant if they change lots of aspects of people's lives.	Comparing events against the same criteria helps us decide which events are the most significant. People choose different criteria because they have different attitudes and values. This means they disagree about who and what is significant.
Diversity	People's lives are different even if they live in the same country in the same period of history.	In history we make generalisations about people because they are a useful way of summing up. It is important to test generalisations and strengthen them to make sure they are as accurate as possible.
Interpretations	People tell different stories of the past. People create different interpretations by including some people, topics or evidence and leaving out or playing down others.	Interpretations are determined by the attitudes and beliefs of the person creating the interpretation. Interpretations can be controversial.

A quick history of Britain 1500–1900

Fill in this grid with answers to the questions in the first column.

	1500	1750	1850	1900
1 What kind of work did people do?				
2 What were their homes like?				
3 What was their religion?				
4 Who was their ruler?				
5 Could they lead healthy lives?				
6 What was the quality of their environment?				

2
Timeline 1400–1900

Use this timeline to complete questions 5 and 6 from page 13.

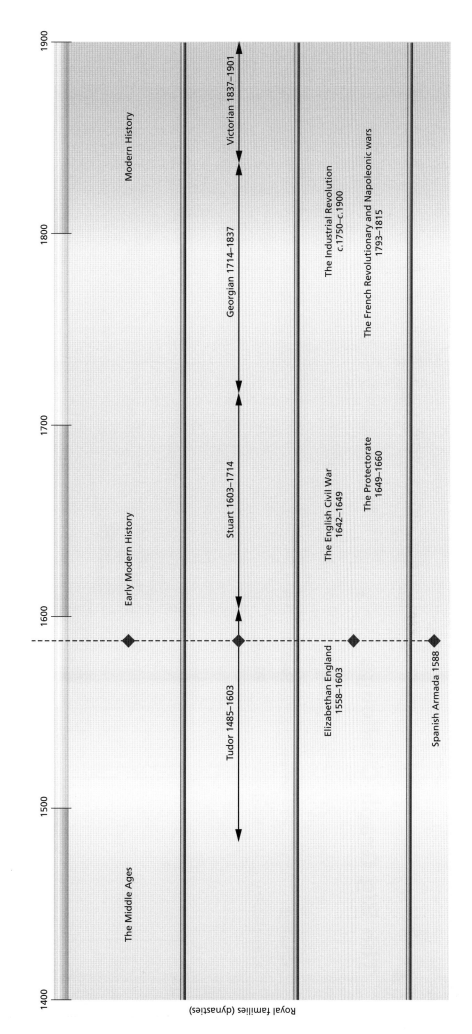

1400   1500   1600   1700   1800   1900

The Middle Ages

Early Modern History

Modern History

Royal families (dynasties)

Tudor 1485–1603

Stuart 1603–1714

Georgian 1714–1837

Victorian 1837–1901

Elizabethan England 1558–1603

The English Civil War 1642–1649

The Industrial Revolution c.1750–c.1900

The Protectorate 1649–1660

The French Revolutionary and Napoleonic wars 1793–1815

Spanish Armada 1588

The Big Graph Challenge

Change	Progress	Rapid
Continuity	Regress	Slow

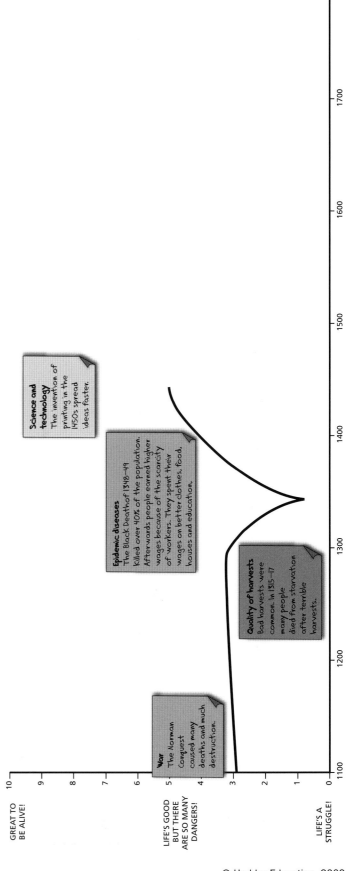

War
The Norman Conquest caused many deaths and much destruction.

Quality of harvests
Bad harvests were common. In 1315–17 many people died from starvation after terrible harvests.

Epidemic diseases
The Black Death of 1348–49 killed over 40% of the population. Afterwards people earned higher wages because of the scarcity of workers. They spent their wages on better clothes, food, houses and education.

Science and technology
The invention of printing in the 1450s spread ideas faster.

GREAT TO BE ALIVE!

LIFE'S GOOD BUT THERE ARE SO MANY DANGERS!

LIFE'S A STRUGGLE!

10
9
8
7
6
5
4
3
2
1
0

1100   1200   1300   1400   1500   1600   1700   1800   1900

1500: Which home would you like to live in?

Use this sheet for the Activity on page 17.

	Which family?	What work did they do?	How did they light their home?	How did they keep clean?	Where did they sleep?	Which family had best standard of living?	The big differences between then and now
Inventory 1							
Inventory 2							
Inventory 3							

Roll up! Roll up! Take a chance on life!

Use this sheet to record what happens to your family at each of the five Moments of Fate.

Name of family	Moment of Fate 1	Moment of Fate 2	Moment of Fate 3	Moment of Fate 4	Moment of Fate 5

The Big Graph Challenge: Part 1, 1500–1750

Use this sheet for question 1 of the Activity on page 23. Complete column 3, describing how life changed between 1500 and 1750.

	Life in 1500	Life in 1750	Continuity or change? A little or a lot of change? Is this aspect better or worse?
HOMES	• Houses and clothing: simple, home-made, but improving. • Food: simple, home-grown. • Education: some children went to school for a year or two.	• Houses and clothing: simple, home-made, but improving. • Food: simple, home-grown. • Education: some children went to school for a year or two.	
WORK & TOWNS	• Most people worked on the land. • There were some small towns. • The only big city was London (population 70,000).	• Most people worked on the land. • There were a few more small towns and cities but only London had got really big (population 657,000).	
LEISURE & TRAVEL	• People had lots of Roman Catholic Church holidays, which were unpaid. • Travel was slow, on foot or horseback.	• Far fewer holidays because Protestant England banned Roman Catholic Church holidays. • Travel was slow, usually on foot, but many roads had been improved by becoming turnpikes (toll roads). Journey times: London to Manchester 4 days; London to Oxford 2 days.	
HEALTH	• Diseases spread easily and there were few cures. • Surgery was extremely risky. • Life expectancy was about 40.	• Diseases spread easily and there were few cures. • Surgery was extremely risky. • Life expectancy was about 40.	

 **7A**

Before and after the Industrial Revolution

This chart shows some of the big changes between 1750 and 1900. Add to it as you work through pages 24–49 of the Pupil's Book.

1750	1900
There were 11 million people in Britain	There were 40 million people in Britain
20% of British people lived in towns	75% of British people lived in towns
Most people were farmers	Most people worked in factories or offices
Most goods were made by hand at home	Most goods were made by machine in factories

7B

Link up the factors

BANKS

Banks were set up to lend money to businesses to help them buy machinery and raw materials.

ENTREPRENEURS

Entrepreneurs were talented and ambitious people who understood how to turn all these different developments into successful businesses to make money.

RAW MATERIALS

Coal was the fuel that powered machines such as steam engines. More cotton, wool and other raw materials were grown to turn into clothing, etc.

TRANSPORT

Better roads, canals and railways carried raw materials to the factories and took away the finished goods for sale.

SOURCES OF POWER

At first water in fast-flowing streams was used to drive machines, then James Watt developed steam engines that were more powerful still.

INVENTORS

Inventors created and improved machines that made more goods more quickly or drove other machines faster.

BRITISH EMPIRE

Countries such as India provided cotton to make into clothes and then bought back the finished goods.

HIGHER POPULATION

More people in Britain meant that more food, clothing and everyday items were needed. The people also provided the workforce for the new industries.

FARMING IMPROVEMENTS

Farmers grew more crops and bigger animals to feed the increasing population.

 **8**

A better life? Manchester in 1850

Use this sheet to help you complete the Activity on page 26.

HOW LIFE IS CHANGING IN THE NEW INDUSTRIAL CITIES: MANCHESTER	
Question	**Answer** (backed up by evidence from which sources?)
Are the homes of the industrial workers good to live in?	
Are workers fairly treated in the factories?	
Is life getting better for the people of Manchester?	

Which three sources will you select to quote or use in your article? Explain why you chose them.

_____

_____

_____

Change and continuity, 1750–1850

Use this sheet to help you with the Activity on page 30.

Use this sheet to help you with the Activity on page 30.

SOURCE 1 Water-powered tilt-hammer, 1772.

SOURCE 2 Steam hammer, 1840.

10 The Big Graph Challenge: Part 2, 1750–1850

Use this sheet for question 1 of the Activity on page 31. Complete column 3, describing how life changed between 1500 and 1750.

	Life in 1750	Life in 1850	Continuity or change? A little or a lot of change? Is this aspect better or worse?
HOMES	• Houses and clothing: simple, home-made, but improving. • Food: simple, home-grown. • Education: some children went to school for a year or two.	• Homes in rural areas still simple. Homes in industrial cities often overcrowded, poorly built, with no running water, drains or toilets. Cheap cotton available.	
WORK & TOWNS	• Most people worked on the land. • There were a few more small towns and cities but only London had got really big (population 657,000).	• Lots of people still worked on the land, but even more now worked in factories, mines and on the railways. • As well as London (now with 2.5m people) many large new cities had grown up in the industrial north and Scotland: Liverpool 376,000; Glasgow 345,000; Manchester 303,000; Birmingham 233,000; Leeds 172,000.	
LEISURE & TRAVEL	• Far fewer holidays because Protestant England banned Roman Catholic Church holidays. • Travel was slow, usually on foot, but many roads had been improved by becoming turnpikes (toll roads). Journey times: London to Manchester 4 days; London to Oxford 2 days.	• Still very few holidays – most people worked a six-day week, with only Christmas off. • Railways connected every major town and city in Britain, making much faster travel available for all. Journey times: London to Manchester 6 hours; London to Oxford 2 hours.	
HEALTH	• Diseases spread easily and there were few cures. • Surgery was extremely risky. • Life expectancy was about 40.	• The unhealthy living conditions in the new industrial cities meant that serious diseases spread easily. There was vaccination against smallpox, but few other cures. • Surgery was extremely risky and life expectancy in some cities was only 35.	

Inside a Victorian photograph album

Use this sheet for the Activity on page 34.

	What does the source show?	Evidence of way life was changing	Evidence of things not changing or getting worse
Source ___			
Source ___			
Source ___			

Learning Log – Doing History: Evidence

Using sources well means:

- Finding things from a source that it doesn't obviously tell you. This is called **inference**.

> **Inference language box**
>
> From .... we can infer that ....
>
> This .... suggests that ....
>
> We can tell from .... that ....
>
> It doesn't say so, but .... must be true because ....

- Checking sources against each other to find ways in which they agree or disagree with each other before deciding on your answer. This is called **cross-referencing**.

> **Cross-reference language box**
>
> This source supports the evidence of Source ...... by ....
>
> If you compare ...., you can tell that ....
>
> This picture shows .... and you can see the same in picture ..., so that
> ....
>
> These pictures show different effects of ....
>
> This source goes even further than Source .... in showing/suggesting ....
>
> This source says ...., but Source .... says ....
>
> This source contradicts Source ...... by ....

- **Selecting** the sources that are most useful for investigating a particular enquiry, or for telling a particular story.

> **Selection language box**
>
> This picture is important because ....
>
> The value of this picture is ....
>
> I chose these two pictures to show different ....
>
> The evidence from this source is convincing because ....
>
> This source is important because it is the only one that ....

Why was ordinary life changing so much?

Use this sheet for question 1 of the Activity on page 45. Write the number of each ball around the correct 'basket' below.

Learning Log – The Big Story: Ordinary Life Part Three

Use this sheet to help you answer the questions in the Learning Log on page 47.

1 Which two periods do you think saw the fastest improvements in ordinary life? Explain what happened in each period.

_____

_____

_____

_____

2 Choose two occasions when ordinary life got worse. Explain how quickly these changes happened.

_____

_____

_____

_____

3 Look at the factors that have affected people's lives. Are there any differences between the factors affecting life before 1750 and those after 1750?

_____

_____

_____

_____

4 What most surprises or interests you about this graph? Explain your reasons.

_____

_____

_____

_____

15

What were they thinking about ... ordinary life?

Use this sheet for the Activity on page 49.

A
Only another week and we can get the harvest in. I pray to God that heavy rain doesn't ruin the crops. Another bad harvest like last year and people will go hungry this winter. Some may even starve to death if the harvest's really bad.

B
It will be back-breaking work bringing the harvest in but there'll soon be time off. There's plenty of Saints' days coming up. One day we'll walk into the nearby town to go to the fair.

C
Thanks be to God for the good monks at the monastery. We can depend on the monks to give us help if there is no work or food prices are high.

D
My cousin died of plague last week. Our priest says God sends plague to punish us for wickedness. Not even Goody Agnes' remedies help us. Our lives are in God's hands.

E
I would like to learn to read but that's only for boys. Father says the priest will teach my brothers for a few hours a week. Mother will teach me how to run the house, make clothes and all the other womanly tasks.

F
I'll be in the fields at sun up tomorrow – or about then. So long as I get the job done nobody minds exactly when I start. It makes for long days in summer but shorter ones in winter.

G
There are rumours that people in other countries are quarrelling over religion. At least in England we all belong to the Catholic Church. Everyone must follow the same beliefs in this country.

H
Life is very different from grandfather's time. People have more chance to get on if they work hard. Most still work in farming but there are new jobs like printing. Maybe that would be something for one of the boys?

I
We've worked hard and earned more money this year. Maybe we'll be able to buy some pewter plates and perhaps some wall-hangings to make our house more cosy.

What were they thinking about ... ordinary life?

Use this sheet for the Activity on page 49.

1
On Sunday mornings we go our separate ways. I am a Catholic but my husband belongs to the Church of England. My neighbours go to the Methodist church. Religion is very important to us but thank heavens we don't burn people any more for being different.

2
My brother tells me it's been another good harvest in his village. Here in the town we just go to the market to buy food. Even if our harvest's not so good there's plenty of food imported from our great Empire, even frozen meat from Australia.

3
I can hear the factory bell. Everyone in the factory has to be there on time; the same time almost every day of the year. If they're late they lose a day's wages.

4

5

6

7

8

9

16

A quick history of European empires

Use these maps for the Activity on page 53. Add your own headline to show how the empires were changing. Write reasons why European countries wanted empires in the boxes below the maps.

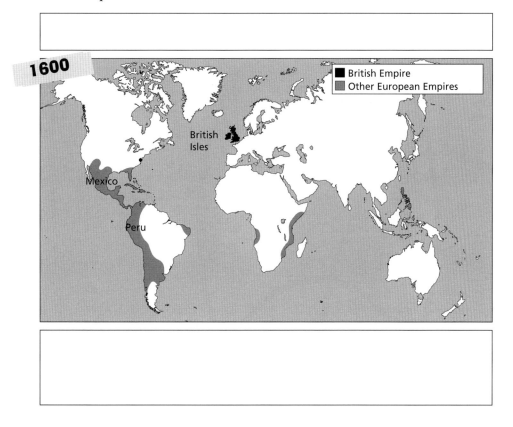

1600

British Empire
Other European Empires

British Isles

Mexico

Peru

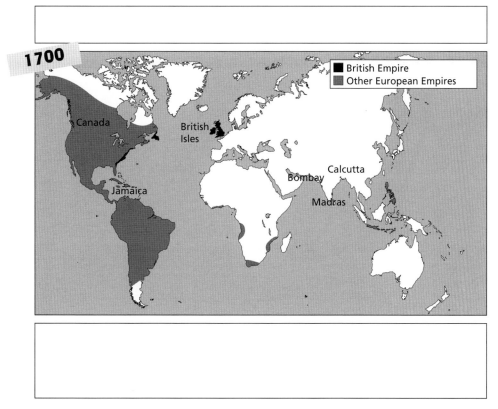

1700

British Empire
Other European Empires

Canada

British Isles

Jamaica

Bombay

Calcutta

Madras

A quick history of European empires

Use these maps for the Activity on page 53. Add your own headline to show how the empires were changing. Write reasons why European countries wanted empires in the boxes below the maps.

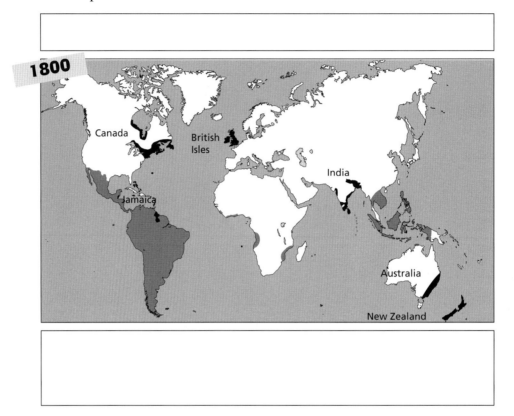

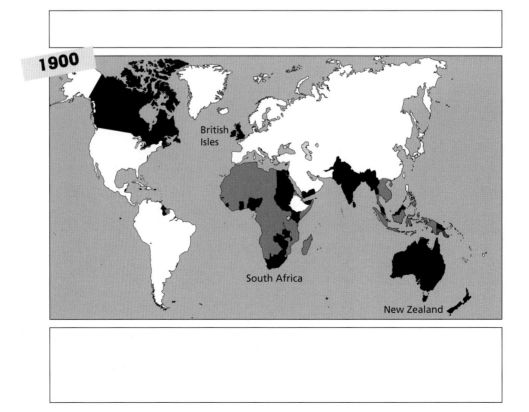

 **17**

How would the Spaniards describe the Aztecs to their friends back in Europe?

Use the windows to record the key points of your report.

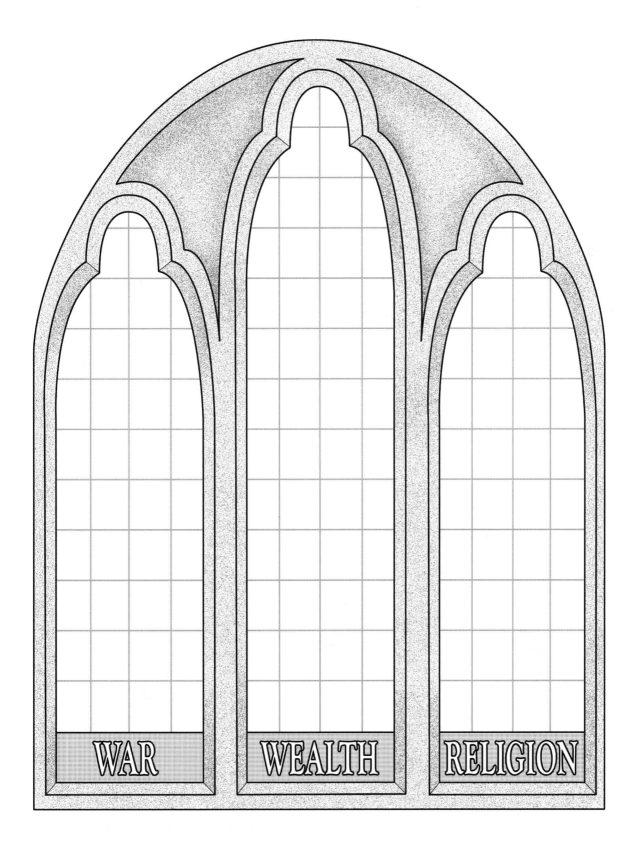

The big questions about empire

Why did the Spanish conquistadors want an empire?

| Roman AND Spanish reasons | ☐ |
| Extra reasons for the conquistadors wanting an empire | ☐ |

The big questions about empire

How did the conquistadors take over and control their empire?

Roman AND Spanish methods	☐
Extra points that apply to Spanish methods of control	☐

19

How did the Spanish conquest of Mexico affect the native people?

Use this sheet to help you complete questions 5 and 6 on page 63.

In the first column, draw a skittle that has fallen, is tottering, or is still upright. In the second column, write the correct label for the skittle and add a brief reason for your decision.

Skittle	Reason
1	
2	
3	
4	
5	
6	
7	
8	
9	
10	

 **20**

Interpretations of the story of Cortes' arrival and conquest of the Aztecs: word bank

First impressions and reception by the Aztecs			
amazement	surprise	uncertain	language
colour	riches	costumes	gold
hospitality	friendly		
buildings	number of people		

Changing attitudes				
culture	traditions	Christian	religion	disgust
sacrifice	blood	cruelty	savage	horror
respect	beliefs	proud		

Fighting and war			
weapons	sword	armour	soldiers
outnumbered	defeat	primitive	victory
fight to the death	brave	courage	fierce

Outcomes			
success	power	wealth	takeover
unfair	disaster	wiped out	disease
landowner	riches	wicked	wrong
treated	slaves		

Emotions			
anger	despair	humiliation	pride
shame	guilt	triumph	pleasure
satisfaction	greed		

The Triangular Trade

Select information from the text on page 71 to add to the boxes for each stage of the journey.

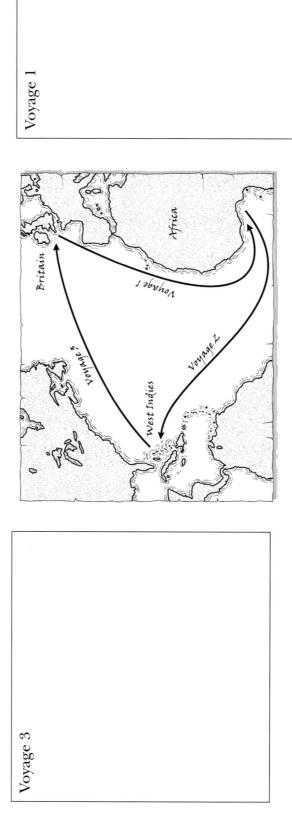

Voyage 1

Voyage 3

Voyage 2

Slavery: who benefited?

Cut out these cards to use on your ripple diagram in the activity on page 73.

African war lords who captured other Africans and sold them to Europeans	The factory owners who exported goods to Africa and the West Indies
British slave ship owners who made up to 50% profit on some voyages	Bankers who did well by lending money to slave traders
British slave traders who bought and sold the slaves	Ordinary people, working at jobs that were dependent on the slave trade, who enjoyed the goods, such as sugar, produced by the slaves
Plantation owners who used slaves, providing only basic food, shelter and no wages	Capitalists who benefited from the profits of slavery that were invested in factories and mines

23

Ripple diagram

Copy this ripple diagram on to a big piece of paper and use it for the Activity on page 73. Then record your decisions on this sheet.

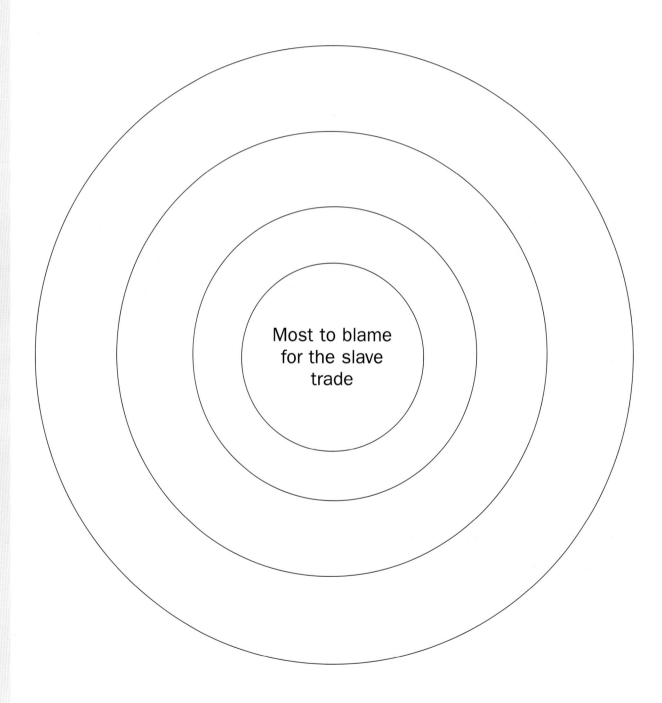

Most to blame
for the slave
trade

 **24**

Arguments in defence of the slave trade: role-play cards

Africans are less skilled than Europeans, proving that white people are superior, so we have a right to do as we wish with black people.	The slave trade makes lots of money for Britain and it must continue. Africa is backward so no other type of trade is possible.
Slaves are not treated cruelly when they are captured in Africa. They are already prisoners of war and would have been killed anyway.	Slaves are treated well on the slave ships. Conditions are good.
African slaves are treated well by their masters on the plantations.	

Evidence found against the defence of the slave trade

Use this chart to help you with the Clarkson Challenge 3 on page 75.

Argument put forward to defend the slave trade	Your counter argument	Supporting evidence	Witness
1 Africans were less skilled than Europeans – white people were superior	African kingdoms before the arrival of Europeans were just as advanced as those in Europe	The Kingdom of Ghana … The Kingdom of Benin …	
2 The slave trade made lots of money for Britain. Africa was undeveloped so no other trade there was possible			
3 Slaves were not captured cruelly			
4 Conditions on the slave ships were good			
5 Enslaved Africans were treated well on the plantations			

26

Proposal table for your documentary

Use this sheet to plan your documentary.

Section and time allowed	Outline
1 ___ mins	
2 ___ mins	
3 ___ mins	
4 ___ mins	
5 ___ mins	
6 ___ mins	
7 ___ mins	
8 ___ mins	
9 ___ mins	
10 ___ mins	

 **27**

Reflections on the British Empire for Victorian schoolchildren

The sun never sets on our Glorious Empire. As Lord Curzon, our Viceroy in India, has said, it "is the greatest force for good the world has ever seen". It contains a quarter of the world's population, including the colonies in the West Indies, in Egypt, in India and in Malaya.

These fortunate people benefit from our fair rule of law, our advanced technology and trade in goods from all corners of the globe.

As a result of our understanding of the cruel and barbaric nature of the Slave Trade and the evils of slavery, these were abolished in all our colonies many years ago.

How wonderful it is to be part of such an Empire.

God save the Queen.

 **28**

The stories of the British Empire

Summarise the evidence you have found out about the British Empire in the table below.

Thumbs up	Open to interpretation	Thumbs down

Why were they mad about empires?

Use the speech bubbles from page 97 to write what each of these people might have said. Some of the speech bubbles you have been given will apply to more than one person.

A Roman general

A Briton who was part of the Roman Empire

An Aztec

A conquistador

A British politician in the 1800s

An Indian woman living in the British Empire in the 1800s

30A

Why did they emigrate?

Use sheets 30A–C to help you with the Activity on page 100.

Look at question 1 on page 100. Copy the four examples into the correct section of your own diagram. Add the reasons why people from each of the case studies emigrated.

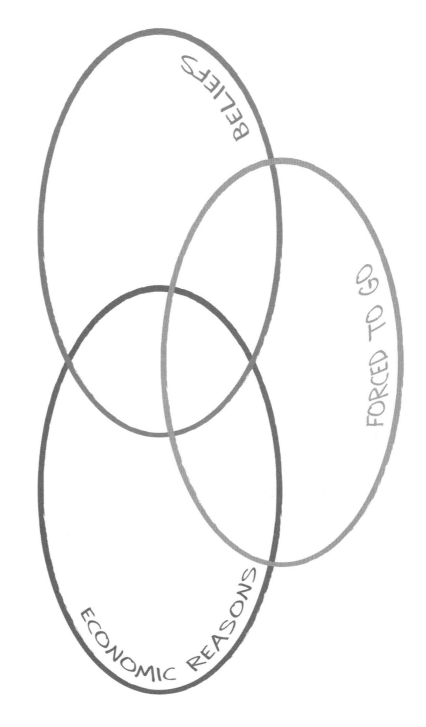

BELIEFS

FORCED TO GO

ECONOMIC REASONS

30B

How were they received in their new land?

Look at question 2 on page 100. Add a label, joined to the diagram below by an arrow, to show where on the scale you think each of the seven groups of people in the examples you have looked at should be.

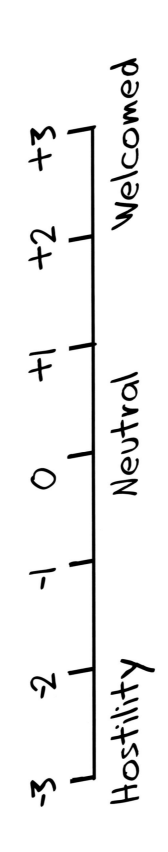

-3 -2 -1 0 +1 +2 +3

Hostility   Neutral   Welcomed

What effects did their arrival have on their new land?

Look at question 3 on page 100. Draw a symbol (don't forget to add a key) or write a label in the correct part of the diagram below for each of the seven examples you have studied.

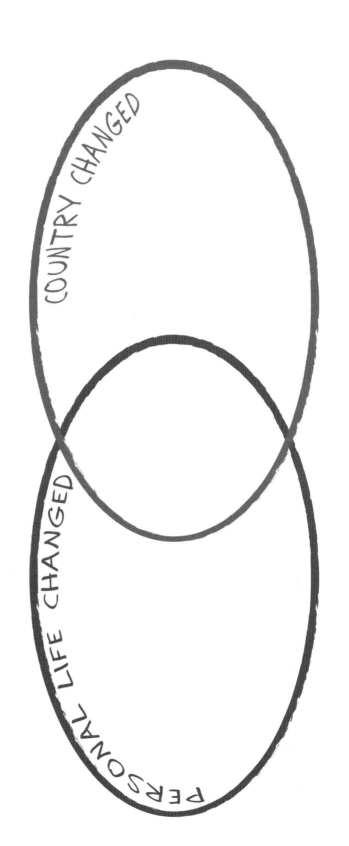

Qualifying words

a few	many
some	majority
minority	often
sometimes	occasionally
probably	possibly
may (be, have)	might (be, have)
partly	unusually

The Big Story: Movement and Settlement Part Two

Empires

Power: monarchy and democracy

Movement and Settlement: the story of emigration

Ordinary Life

Conflicts

 **33**

Why did William's invasion succeed?

Use this sheet for the Activity on page 113. Choose a good reason for William's success to end each of your cards. Be careful! Some of the suggestions in the boxes below are wrong, or do not fit any of the cards.

Planning
William's plans were …

Weapons
The Normans had better …

Fighting Forces
The English army was …

Leadership
William's leadership was …

Luck
The weather helped …

… tired, having marched south after defeating Harald Hardrada.

… Harold because William didn't like the rain in England but the English were used to it.

… carefully made and included building hundreds of ships for the journey to England.

… inspiring for his men because he led them bravely into battle and chose a clever tactic, when he pretended to retreat.

… ready and waiting for William when he landed at Pevensey Bay.

… cannons so they could shoot at Harold from France.

… William because the wind turned to blow him across the Channel at exactly the time Harold was fighting in the north.

… weapons because they had archers and used horses, though Harold's men held the shield wall against them until the very end of the battle.

… rather hurried and disorganised because he wanted to sail before the wind changed again.

Why did the Spanish invasion fail?

Use this writing frame to help write up the reasons for the failure of the Armada.

Copy and complete the introduction below, using your own words to fill in the spaces.

In _____, King Philip II of Spain decided to invade _____ because he wanted to remove _____ from the throne and put a new, Roman _____ ruler in her place. However, his planned _____ did not succeed.

Now write one paragraph for each of the five factors you have been investigating, including some information from each card to support the point you are making. Try to explain links between the factors. Use the paragraph starters below to help you organise your ideas.

One reason for Philip's failure was ... (Choose one of the factors – planning, leadership, fighting forces, weapons or luck – and explain why that did not work in Philip's favour.) *An example of this was ...* (Use evidence to support your point.)

This links with another reason why the Armada was not successful, which was ... (Choose a different factor, explain how the two factors are connected and how the second factor contributed to the failure of the Armada, supporting the point with evidence.)

Write one paragraph for each of the remaining three factors, making links between them when you can. Use the phrases below to help you.

A further problem for the Spanish was ...

This led to ...

Also, ...

In addition, ...

These reasons are linked because ...

A final factor that stopped Philip's invasion was ...

Finish your answer with a short conclusion. This should sum up what you think is/are the most important reason/s why the invasion failed. There may be one thing that you feel led to all the others or you may feel it was a combination of all or several of the factors.

Therefore/Overall, the Spanish invasion of England failed because ...

Was Nelson the main reason why Napoleon's invasion failed?

Use this writing frame to write up the reasons why Napoleon failed to invade England and decide if Nelson's leadership was the most important factor.

Copy and complete the introduction below, using your own words to fill in the spaces.

In _____, Emperor Napoleon Bonaparte decided to invade _____ because he

wanted to increase his _____. The _____ government was very worried and

they organised the building of _____ Towers to defend the south coast. However, the

planned _____ did not succeed.

Then write one paragraph for each of the five factors you have been investigating, including some information from each card to support the point you are making. Try to explain links between the factors. Use the paragraph starters below to help you organise your ideas.

One reason for Napoleon's defeat was leadership . . . (Choose this factor first because it is the main point of the question.) *This was important because ...*

An example of good/bad leadership was ....

The leadership factor links with ... (Choose a different factor – planning, fighting forces, weapons or luck) *which is another reason why Napoleon was not successful.* (Explain how the two factors are connected and how the second factor contributed to French failure, supporting the point with evidence.)

Write one paragraph for each of the remaining three factors, making links between them when you can. Use the phrases below to help you.

A further problem for Napoleon was ...

This led to ...

Also, ...

In addition, ...

These reasons are linked because ...

A final factor that stopped the French invasion was ...

Finish your answer with a short conclusion. This should sum up what you think, saying either that you agree that Nelson was the main reason the invasion failed and his role led to all Napoleon's other problems, or suggesting that there were other factors that were equally or more important.

Therefore/Overall, the most important reason/s for Napoleon's failure to invade England was/were ... and/so Nelson ...

How significant are these wars?

Copy the four criteria your group has chosen into the boxes on the top row of the grid below. Decide if you want to adjust the weighting for each criterion, giving up to 5 extra points for the most important one/s and only 1 or 2 points for criteria you think are less significant.

Use the Top Trump cards or your own judgement to give a score out of 10 for each war, measured against each criterion.

Criterion				
Weighting				
Henry VIII's wars with Scotland				
Elizabeth I and the Armada				
Elizabeth I's wars with Ireland				
Anglo-Dutch war				
Marlborough's Wars				
Bonnie Prince Charlie's Rebellion				
War of Jenkins' Ear				
Seven Years War				
War of American Independence				
Napoleonic Wars				
Opium Wars				
Crimean War				
Sikh Wars				
Afghan Wars				
Zulu War				
Boer War				

 **37**

How were ideas and beliefs about war changing?

Use this sheet for the Activity on page 138.

1500	1600	1700	1800	1900

	It is important to stop one country taking control of the whole of Europe. If necessary we will make alliances to stop any country dominating Europe.

	We have a right to build up an overseas empire and trade all over the world. There is only so much wealth in the world to share so we will fight other countries to defend and increase our share of empire and trade.

Having a strong navy is vital for defending Britain against invasion and for defending our Empire and trade throughout the world.

England needs to go to war to take control of the rest of Britain.

The king needs to go to war to show his people how powerful he is.		Britain has become the richest nation in the world because of its empire and trade, so it needs to fight wars to protect them.

	We do not want another country to tell us what our religion should be.		We cannot afford to let other countries build up industrial strength to match our own. This will threaten the British Empire and make us weaker in wars.

How were ideas and beliefs about war changing?

Use this sheet for the Activity on page 138.

A England successfully fought off the Spanish Armada in 1588.	**G** During the French Revolutionary Wars and Napoleonic Wars (1793–1815) Britain made a series of alliances with other countries in Europe.
B Britain won the Opium Wars against China in the mid-nineteenth century.	**H** During the 1800s Britain produced far more iron and steel than any other country. The industries were able to make weapons in wartime and the textile industries produced uniforms and other equipment. Britain's wealth played a big part in defeating Napoleon's France.
C John Churchill, Duke of Marlborough, commanded the British forces who, with their allies, defeated the French in the late 1600s and 1700s.	**I** The key turning point at the Battle of Waterloo in 1815 was the arrival of the Prussian army to fight alongside the British forces.
D The Seven Years War (1756–1763) between Britain and France was the first worldwide war with battles in North America and India as well as Europe.	**J** Twice in the 1800s Britain tried to take control of Afghanistan in order to stop Russia threatening Britain's empire in India.
E Henry VIII invaded France, wanting to be as famous a hero as Henry V. He failed.	**K** By the late 1800s Germany, France and the USA were matching Britain's industrial strength and were developing new methods for producing goods more cheaply and efficiently.
F Nelson's victory at the Battle of Trafalgar in 1805 ended the threat of French invasion.	**L** Henry VIII spent a great deal of money on his wars with Scotland.

38A

Would you have signed Charles I's death warrant?

Read the information from pages 142–143. Record in the table all the things that King Charles I did wrong, relating to the charge that he ignored Parliament, and all the points that Charles would have made in his own defence. You could group the ideas and rule off between them to make your record clearer.

Charge	Evidence against Charles	Charles' defence
1 'That he did ignore the will of Parliament and ruled according to his own will'		

38B

Would you have signed Charles I's death warrant?

Read the information from pages 144–145. Record in the table all the things that King Charles I did wrong, relating to the charge that he made war on his own subjects. You should also record all the points that Charles would have made in his own defence.

Charge	Evidence against Charles	Charles' defence
2 ' ... that he did wickedly make war on his own subjects ...'		

Would you have signed Charles I's death warrant?

Read the information from pages 146–148. Record in the table all the things that King Charles I did wrong, relating to the charge that he was responsible for all the damage and desolation, and to the charge that he restarted the war after being defeated. You should also record all the points that Charles would have made in his own defence.

Charge	Evidence against Charles	Charles' defence
3 ... that he was responsible for all the murders, rapings, burnings, damage and desolation caused by the wars		
4 ... that he restarted the war after being defeated		

Glossary of important words and phrases

Match the words and phrases on the left to the correct meaning and copy them into your book.

'The Divine Right of Kings'	The most important landowners, often called barons or lords, and the most important Churchmen in Britain
The role of Parliament	The idea that the King has been appointed by God and so rules by God's authority
Taxes	The place where MPs met to discuss and make laws and agree taxes for the monarch
Nobles and bishops	Members of Parliament – not nobles or bishops but, in the seventeenth century, still rich and important men
House of Commons	Money collected from the population, with the permission of Parliament, for the monarch (or government) to use for ruling the country
MPs	The main task of Parliament in Charles I's time was to grant taxes to the King, but Parliament also expected to be consulted by the King about important decisions

 **39B**

The trial of King Charles I – a play

Use the following 5-page script to act out the events of January 1649.

Characters	**Non-speaking parts**
Narrator	Two guards
John Bradshaw – President of the Court	Up to twelve judges
Simon Moore – The Clerk to the Court	Several soldiers
King Charles	Several spectators
Caroline Sweet – First spectator	
Jane Davis – Second spectator	
Gerald Baxter – Parliamentarian soldier	
Francis Hale – Parliamentarian soldier	
Veronica Maunders – Servant at Carisbrooke Castle	

Act One. Scene 1. Westminster Hall.

The First Day: Saturday 20 January 1649
Everyone files slowly into the room

Clerk to the Court	Will you all take your seats please. Soldiers down both sides of the hall. Spectators at the far end. Quickly now. Make way for John Bradshaw, the President of the Court, and the rest of the judges.
John Bradshaw	*(striding through)* You're doing a fine job, my friend. Today is the most important day in the history of England. Today a king is to be tried for treason. In 300 years' time, people will read about this day and will praise us for what we have done.
Narrator	Everyone took their rightful places and then silence fell. The story began in 1642, when King Charles and his Royalist army went to war with the Parliamentarian army. The Royalists lost the war and King Charles was sent to prison in Carisbrooke Castle. He started plotting with the Scots and tried to persuade them to invade England. There was a second civil war which the King also lost. Now it is January 1649, and King Charles is being tried for treason.
Clerk to the Court	Bring the prisoner to the dock. *(Two guards appear, one on either side of the King. Slowly they lead him to the dock)*
Caroline Sweet	*(Leans over to her friend)* Just look at him. He's so thin and grey.
Jane Davis	Serves him right! All the pain and torment he's caused us. I've lost my husband and two sons thanks to this war.

Playscript: page 2

Caroline Sweet	I know, but after all he is our King. He looks like a man who has suffered, doesn't he? Just look at his eyes. They look lost. I think he knows what is going to happen to him.
Jane Davis	A fair trial and a fair result. That's what will happen to him. He'll go to the block and none deserves it more than him!
Clerk to the Court	Silence in court.
Narrator	Everyone turned to look at President Bradshaw. He had a piece of paper in his hand. He looked straight at King Charles and began to read:
John Bradshaw	Charles Stuart, King of England, Scotland and Wales, trusted to use your power for the good of the people; you stand accused of overthrowing the rights and freedom of the people, taking away the power of Parliament, and making war against Parliament and the people. How do you plead? Innocent or guilty?
King Charles	I refuse to answer to these charges. Neither you *(pointing at Bradshaw)* nor anyone else in this room has any legal right to put me on trial.
Narrator	After this, there was an uproar. Spectators started shouting and Bradshaw turned to consult the judges on either side of him. Eventually the Clerk to the Court spoke.
Clerk to the Court	I call this session to an end. We will meet again on Monday at the same time.

Scene 2. Westminster Hall.

The Second Day: Monday 22 January 1649

Narrator	The day began just as Saturday had, with Bradshaw speaking. King Charles was even more angry.
John Bradshaw	Charles Stuart, you are guilty of all the treasons, murders, burnings, damages and mischiefs to this nation committed in the wars. How do you plead?
King Charles	Parliament is not a court of law.
John Bradshaw	Confess or deny the charge.
King Charles	By what authority do you sit?
John Bradshaw	Take him away. *(The two guards lead the King out of the courtroom)*

Playscript: page 3

Scene 3. Westminster Hall.

Witnesses are called

Narrator	The same thing happened on the third day of the trial. After this, the judges banned Charles from coming to the court. They began calling witnesses to accuse Charles of various crimes.
Clerk to the Court	I call Gerald Baxter to bear witness to the court.
John Bradshaw	And what have you got to say?
Gerald Baxter	*(stammering)* I was there, Sir, on that dreadful day in August 1642. King Charles, Sir, he was dead set on war. We tried to stop him but he wouldn't listen. He raised his standard at Nottingham and started the whole sorry business.
John Bradshaw	Thank you for your honourable testimony. Now who have we next? Ah yes, Francis Hale. What have you got to tell us? *(Francis Hale is led forward)*
Francis Hale	I started the war siding with the King, your Honour. But then I got sickened by the way he treated prisoners after we'd captured Leicester. Why, I swear by God's own holy breath that he said 'I do not care if they cut them three times more, for they are mine enemies!'
Narrator	There were horrified murmurs from the spectators. Even Bradshaw looked shocked. The Clerk to the Court called the final witness.
Clerk to the Court	I call the final witness for the prosecution. Veronica Maunders.
Veronica Maunders	*(producing a crumpled piece of paper in her hand)* Your 'ighness, I swear I am only a poor servant at Carisbrooke Castle but I knows an evil man when I sees one! When Charles was prisoner in the castle, he asked me to deliver this letter secretly. I knew it was wrong. Not that I can read, you understand. But I took it straight to my husband who told me to take it to the Justice.
Narrator	The letter was read out to the court. It showed that while Charles had supposedly been trying to make peace with Parliament, he was secretly asking his son to raise another army to fight again.

Playscript: page 4

Scene 4. Westminster Hall.

Verdict and sentence: Saturday 27 January 1649

Narrator	On 27 January, the court sat again and Charles was brought before the judges for the verdict and sentence. Charles was promised he could make a speech before the verdict was read out.
King Charles	Mr President, I want to talk to my people. Let me speak to the House of Commons and the House of Lords. I have a plan for peace.
John Bradshaw	You had time enough to speak to the Commons and Lords before the war. But you chose to close Parliament down. I forbid you to speak to them now.
King Charles	If you won't let me speak to the Commons and the Lords, at least let me speak to all the people gathered in here.
John Bradshaw	You refused to answer our charges at the beginning of the trial. You have lost your opportunity now. It is too late. This is the sentence that the court has passed upon you. Charles Stuart, King of England, Scotland and Wales, you are guilty of failing in your duty to see that parliaments were called. You have attacked the basic liberties of this country. Therefore … this court does judge that Charles Stuart, a tyrant, traitor, murderer and public enemy of the people, shall be put to death by the severing of his head from his body. *(There is a huge gasp from the people in the courtroom, then a deathly hush)*
Narrator	The execution was fixed for 30 January. The death warrant still had to be signed. In the end less than half of the original 132 judges signed it. The others refused.

Playscript: page 5

Act Two. Scene 1. The Scaffold at Whitehall.

(Crowds are milling around the scaffold, where there is an axeman's block and two guards, one with an axe in his hand)

Narrator   On the morning of 30 January Charles rose early. He asked for two shirts since it was cold and he did not want to appear to be shivering from fear. He was then taken to Whitehall, where he ate a piece of bread and drank some wine and then prayed. At two o'clock he stepped on to the scaffold.

(King Charles is led into the room. He walks up to the block, kneels down and the executioner slowly raises his axe. As the axe falls [careful here!] the crowd groans, cries, moans and shouts. They all rush forward to surround the body)

Narrator   The souvenir hunters rushed to dip their handkerchiefs in the dead king's blood and to take hairs from his head and beard. Then the soldiers came charging in to force the crowd to leave. Everyone ran for their lives.

The next day, King Charles's head was sewn back on to his body. A few days later, the body was quietly buried at Windsor Castle.

Oliver Cromwell – hero or villain?
How attitudes have changed towards him at different times

Use the information from pages 172–173 to find out how attitudes towards Cromwell have changed. Complete the graph below and annotate with your 'thumbs up' and 'thumbs down' symbols.

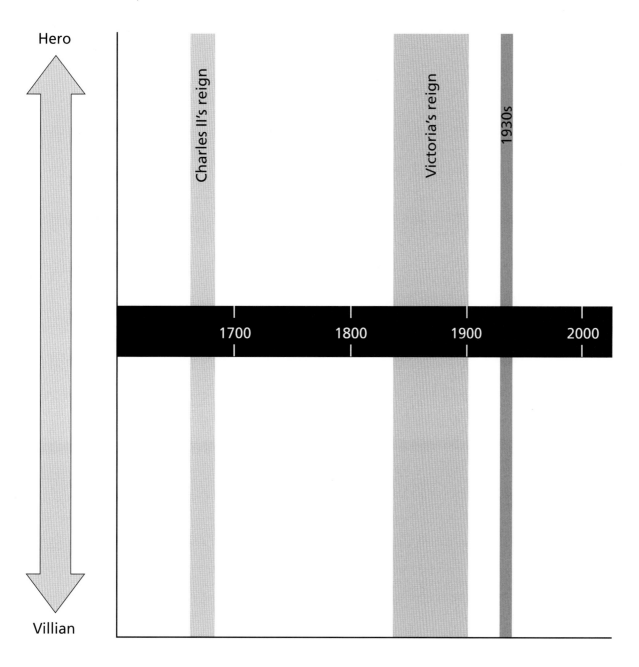

 **41**

Declaration of Independence

Use page 179 to challenge each of the statements below with part of the Declaration of Independence.

The Importance of the Declaration of Independence

1. People are not equal

2. Ordinary people do not have any rights

3. Kings get their power direct from God

4. The upper classes run the government because they own lots of land

5. Rebellion is a sin and a 'treason', which is the worst form of crime

42

The structure of society in France in the 1780s

Use the names for the sections of French society and the descriptions to go with them, from the table below, to complete the labels under each picture.

The Church (Bishops, priests, monks and nuns)	Most were very poor and earned low wages
The Nobility, who owned about 30% of the land	Rich and powerful, with great control over ideas
The Bourgeois (middle classes, including merchants, lawyers and bankers)	Many were starving but had to pay rent to nearly everyone else
The Sans-culottes, city workers	Did not have to pay taxes but collected rent from the peasants
The Peasants, who lived in the countryside and worked on the land	Important for France's prosperity but not allowed to vote

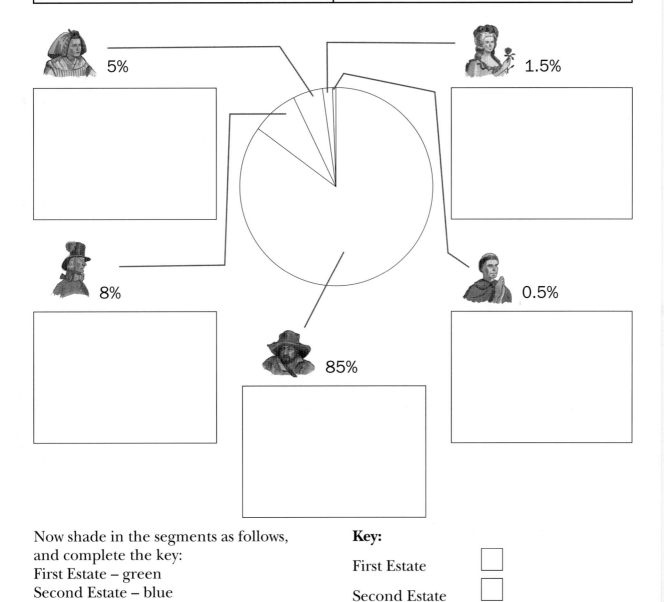

5%

1.5%

8%

0.5%

85%

Now shade in the segments as follows, and complete the key:
First Estate – green
Second Estate – blue
Third Estate – red (note: there are three segments that belong here).

Key:

First Estate ☐

Second Estate ☐

Third Estate ☐

43

Revolution Chart

Use the information from pages 184–191 to complete two copies of the Revolution Chart below.

You will need to write the dates for each chart after the title. The first chart is for the period 1786–1791 and the second for 1791–1815.

REVOLUTION CHART: Date _____

	Aims What did they want?	**Methods** Did they use peaceful or violent methods to achieve their aims?	**Outcomes** What were the consequences? Did s/he get what s/he wanted?
Henri, the bourgeois			
Edith, the sans- culotte			
Gaston, the peasant			

44
The Power-ometer

Use this sheet to help you with the Activity on page 192.

Look at the Power-ometer below. Colour each of the segment labels naming parts of French society in a different colour. As you read the information about the progress of the French Revolution mark how the power swings from one group to another by drawing 7 pointers onto your Power-ometer, matching the colour of the pointer to the social group it indicates. Label each pointer with the correct date. The pointer for a) has already been drawn but you must add the colour and the date.

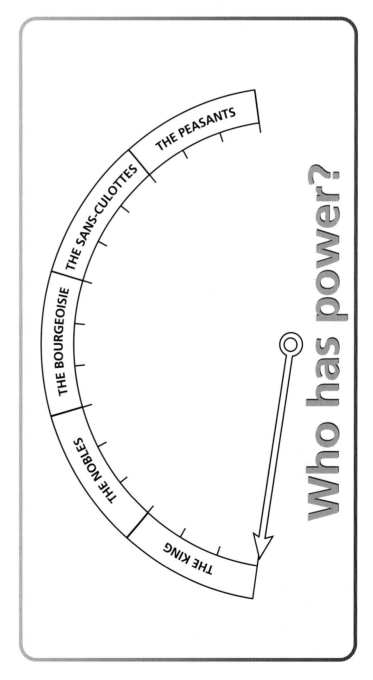

THE PEASANTS

THE SANS-CULOTTES

THE BOURGEOISIE

THE NOBLES

THE KING

Who has power?

45

Causes and consequences of the French Revolution

Use this sheet to help you with Activity 2 on page 192.

Sort the cards below into causes and consequences. Then spread out the consequence cards on a large sheet of paper and draw lines to show how they can link up.

A bourgeois National Assembly took over governing France	France was at war with much of Europe
France was declared a republic	Governments in other countries cracked down on protesters for fear of a revolution
During the Terror, thousands of opponents of the Revolution were executed	Louis XVI did not have enough money to run France
Louis XVI called a meeting of the Estates General	Many French people lived in great poverty
Many sans-culottes and peasants were better off	Napoleon crowned himself Emperor of France
Nobles lost their power and wealth	Peasants in the Vendée rebelled, leading to thousands of deaths
Poor and powerless people in other countries were inspired to protest	Revolutionary ideas spread from France to other countries
The American Declaration of Independence gave other countries a thirst for liberty	The Declaration of the Rights of Man was published
The French King and Queen were executed	

46

Memo to Mr William Pitt, Prime Minister of Great Britain

Write a memo to the Prime Minister, warning him of the dangers that face Britain because of the ideas spreading from Revolutionary France. Use the sentence starters and word bank below to help you. You could also use some of the vocabulary in Source 1 on page 195.

Finish your memo by suggesting what the Prime Minister should do to stop the English from copying the French example.

To The Right Honourable Mr William Pitt, Prime Minister of Britain,

In your own best interests, I am writing to warn you that ...

There are people in this country who are also ...

You will be aware that ...

Britain has become prosperous through trade but ...

Even people who used to be religious ...

Dangerous, revolutionary ideas are being ...

You must ... so that the people of this country ...

In the hope that you will heed this warning, I am your humble servant ...

WORD BANK

The following words may give you some ideas and help with spelling. You do not have to use them all.

violence	horror	destruction	caused by	revolutionary ideas
	poorest citizens	opportunity	freedom	
same rights as others		resulting in	murder	guillotined
victim	savage	prevent	buying and selling	abandon
	trusted	leaflet	booklet	propaganda	intending to
supporters	prevent	spreading further		circulation
	influenced	encouraged		

47A

What was wrong with British elections?

Use this sheet to help you with the activity on page 198.

Major problems	How it should be changed	Why the government might oppose this

47B

What can we learn from history? Did British protesters get what they wanted?

Use this chart for the Activity on page 201.

	Aims What did the protestors want?	**Actions** Did they use peaceful or violent methods to achieve their aims?	**Outcomes** What were the consequences of what they did? Did they get what they wanted?	**Lessons from history** What evidence could James or Sarah use in their speeches?
Peterloo protestors in 1819				
Reform riots of 1831				
The Chartists				

 **48**

What have you learned about sources?

Use this table to record what type of sources are shown on pages 214–215.

	Surviving buildings	Objects	Pictures	Writing	Photographs
'Early Modern period' 1500–1750					
'Industrial period' 1750–1900					
Source not available until after 1900					

49

What have you learned about significance?

Use this sheet for the Activity on page 218. Annotate, highlight or cross out the stamps to help you make your selection of five significant events or people. Think carefully about the criteria you are using to decide what is significant.

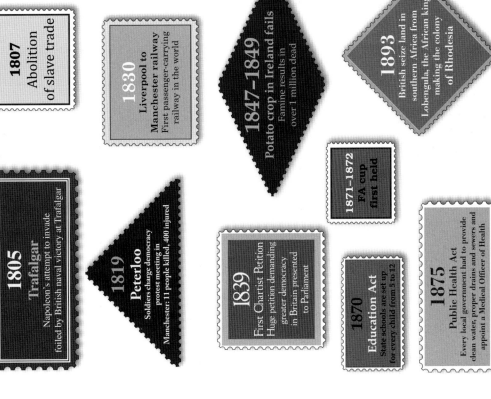

1807 Abolition of slave trade

1830 Liverpool to Manchester railway First passenger-carrying railway in the world

1847–1849 Potato crop in Ireland fails Famine results in over 1 million dead

1893 British seize land in southern Africa from Lobengula, the African king, making the colony of Rhodesia

1805 Trafalgar Napoleon's attempt to invade foiled by British naval victory at Trafalgar

1819 Peterloo Soldiers charge democracy protest meeting in Manchester: 11 people killed, 400 injured

1871–1872 FA cup first held

1839 First Chartist Petition Huge petition demanding greater democracy in Britain presented to Parliament

1870 Education Act State schools are set up for every child from 5 to 12

1875 Public Health Act Every local government had to provide clean water, proper drains and sewers and appoint a Medical Officer of Health

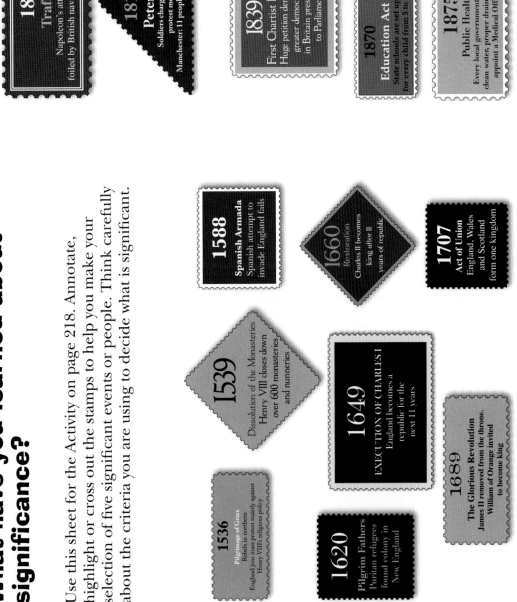

1588 Spanish Armada Spanish attempt to invade England fails

1660 Restoration Charles II becomes king after 11 years of republic

1707 Act of Union England, Wales and Scotland form one kingdom

1539 Dissolution of the Monasteries Henry VIII closes down over 600 monasteries and nunneries

1649 EXECUTION OF CHARLES I England becomes a republic for the next 11 years

1689 The Glorious Revolution James II removed from the throne, William of Orange invited to become king

1536 Pilgrimage of Grace Rebels in northern England join mass protest mainly against Henry VIII's religious policy

1620 Pilgrim Fathers Puritan refugees found colony in New England

50

Can you make connections?

Use this sheet to help you with the Activity on page 223. Draw the links you have made between the different themes, then 'hang' the connecting evidence on each line.

Monarchy

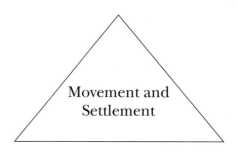

Democracy

Empire

Ordinary
Life

Conflict